The 101 Club

The inspirational story of

HUDDERSFIELD TOWN's

record-breaking **1979-80** season

To Nathan
Best Wishes

by

Rob Stewart

Foreword by

Dean Hoyle

To Nathon

GREAT NORTHERN

Great Northern Books Limited
PO Box 1380, Bradford, BD5 5FB
www.greatnorthernbooks.co.uk

ISBN: 978-1-912101-55-9 (Paperback Edition)

Design and layout: David Burrill

CIP Data
A catalogue for this book is available from the British Library

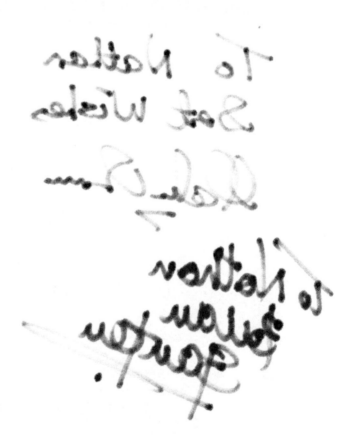

The 101 Club

Rob Stewart was brought up on Huddersfield's Walpole Road council estate before heading off to York University. After spells on the *Holmfirth Express* and *Hull Daily Mail*, he went it alone as a freelance journalist and spent a decade as a football reporter for *The Daily Telegraph*. He now covers football for national newspapers and is a regular contributor to *Four Four Two* magazine and *Backpass*. He lives with his partner and three children in exile in Bristol.

Foreword

by Dean Hoyle

Just as David Wagner and our current players will be the heroes of a generation, Mick Buxton and his players are mine.

The promotion season that Rob has written about so eloquently got me hooked on football, specifically Huddersfield Town, so I'm proud to write the foreword for his book on a special team.

I grew up in Heckmondwike, so in football terms I could have turned right to Leeds or left for Huddersfield. I don't like walking uphill, so it was always going to be Huddersfield! In all seriousness it was my friend, Graham Johnson, who got me on the bus to go to Huddersfield, past the old ICI chemical works.

I can remember the feel and experience of my first match days from that season even now, like it was yesterday. Standing on the terrace with lots of grown men was completely new and exciting to me; the smell of pipes being smoked all around me was really something! Huddersfield Town was – and still is – a traditional, honest, hard-working club; one that was instantly close to my heart.

I loved the 1979/80 team, too. I was very lucky to see such a good, attacking team so young into my days as a supporter; 101 league goals! Ian Robins and Peter Fletcher terrorised defences in Division Four that year; Steve Kindon was electric, Dave Cowling could really cross a ball. Mally Brown, Keith Hanvey, Brian Stanton; I could go on and on.

After one of the Club's lowest ebbs in its long, proud history, Mick, his coaching team and the players reinvigorated the town and gave our fans a season that still lives long in the memory now. For that, we'll be eternally grateful to them all.

For those who weren't part of that thrilling 1979/80 season when we won that Division Four title, it's hard to explain the unique appeal of that squad. No other squad has ever been spoken about with such affection. There were so many larger-than-life characters who, as the *Examiner's* Sports Editor Mel Booth put so well in a recent piece, were as famed for getting into trouble with the authorities as for their ability on the field!

I see similarities in that team and our class of 2017 – on the pitch, thankfully! Mick had us playing an intense, pressing game 45 years ago; the hallmark of David Wagner's side now. Like now, we looked like the fittest team in the league and that goes a long way.

I've come to know Micky through his visits to the Club to watch games - he still makes it whenever his work and travel allows – and when I ask him what he thinks of our style of football now, he always says: "Only the same as I did in 1979!"

In fact, many of the faces from that championship-winning team have become regulars at the Club. I think that's important. We held a reunion for the team in February 2016 and, unsurprisingly to me, it was packed to the rafters at the John Smith's Stadium.

After the Play-Off Final win in May 2017, I called Mick. I wanted the chance to say thank you to him. He said: "Why, what have I done?" And I said: "If it wasn't for you getting me hooked in '79, I would have never have had the best day of my life." He's a proud, strong, Geordie man, but I could tell he was quite touched.

I meant every word, too. Without Mick and the team getting me hooked on Town, I probably wouldn't have had the chance to become Chairman and experienced all the ups – and downs – in charge of my football club.

Football moves quickly and I'm immensely proud to see my team in the Premier League for the first time – but that Division Four season will always have a special place in my heart.

Dean Hoyle
Chairman, Huddersfield Town

Introduction

5.53pm Monday, May 29, 2017

By all accounts, your whole life flashes before you when you're just about to die but something eerily similar happened to me at Wembley Stadium and I've lived to tell this tale.

It was a bizarre sequence of events that occurred in a few magical, shimmering moments high up in the stands at the national stadium and it wasn't because I feared I was about to kick the bucket.

Instead, it all happened at the height of one of the best days of my life as hitherto long-lost images were suddenly cascading after Christopher Schindler's penalty kick had hit the back of the net and sent Huddersfield Town, my humble, little hometown club, into the Premier League for the first time.

I admit it sounds really peculiar but once the ball had travelled past Ali Al-Habsi in the Reading goal, it felt like more than 40 years' worth of memories of watching Town through thick and thin had come rushing back to me all at once.

It was all happening at an unnaturally fast speed as pandemonium broke out all around me and then the inevitable happened and I broke down and burst into tears.

It was all part of the most surreal and unforgettable personal experience and I know that Terriers everywhere will have their own version of a spectacularly curious day.

For the first time in my 50-odd years I got a 'now or never' feeling after Danny Ward had dived down to his left to save Jordan Obita's penalty in the shoot-out. We were within touching distance of something extraordinary and didn't know whether to laugh or cry.

Town were on the cusp of glory and my legs went all hollow as, being a tad superstitious, I had to weigh up whether I should stay sat down or stand back up and whether my decision to dare watch German centre-back Schindler try to hold his nerve and beat Al-Habsi with his spot-kick might influence events.

It was just like being a schoolkid again in the days when I used to watch Leeds United before I saw the light in the build-up to the 1979/80 Fourth Division title winners and took my place in the Cowshed.

And so when Schindler did squeeze the ball beyond Al-Habsi there was that head-rush as all my yesterdays flooded back and those flickering images reminded me that this was one of those things that were not supposed to happen, which of course, is what made the whole thing a lot, lot better.

It was all happening. All sorts of flashbacks got me going right from seeing Town sporting plain blue shirts in the mid-70s while we bumped along at the bottom of the old Fourth Division.

On a happier note, my first Town match – a 2-2 draw under Leeds Road floodlights against QPR in 1972 – was there in my mind's eye but so too were painful memories.

These included a 3-0 Elland Road stuffing by a John Sheridan-inspired Leeds in my university days to the night I was physically sick as Peterborough knocked us out of the play-offs.

It was as if I was hallucinating when all sorts of happy memories came from nowhere and surfaced such as the recent wins over Leeds, the penalty shoot-out victory over Sheffield Wednesday and the play-off final wins over Bristol Rovers and Sheffield United.

And I saw the rest of my football-supporting life flash before me as well with pictures of Town playing at Anfield, Old Trafford and the Emirates in my mind's eye as well as those of people like Paul Pogba and Jose Mourinho heading along Leeds Road.

It was only when my 15-year-old son, Fred, grabbed me as we sat high in the upper tier that I came to my senses before the blubbering began again (and I briefly wondered why the two people next to me had vanished when extra-time ended).

But the most poignant re-collection that popped up was the day in May 1979 when I saw another piece of history unfold right before my very eyes as I stood in the Cowshed alongside schoolmate Michael Lenihan and together we witnessed euphoria for the first time in our lives.

That was down to Mick Buxton's Town team that not only won the old Fourth Division title in dramatic fashion but also did so in style by scoring 101 goals in 46 games.

Town won seven of their last eight games to beat Walsall to silverware with Ian Robins rounding off the campaign in perfect style by scoring the two goals that secured victory over Hartlepool in front of 16,807 of us Terriers.

The 101 Club is my attempt to tell the story of one of the greatest seasons in Huddersfield Town's history, which is saying something for a club that won the Football League three times in a row.

There will be a few raised eyebrows but that stands up to scrutiny because manager Mick Buxton and his squad of 16 players gave Town fans something to shout about after a decade dominated by decay and dismay in the shadowlands of English football.

Town began the decade by winning promotion to the First Division but then suffered a harrowing, record-breaking decline that saw the club slump to second-bottom of the entire 92-club Football League before Buxton grabbed the ailing football club by the scruff of the neck and played the role of saviour to perfection.

They were and still are idols of mine and so I always suspected that Buxton's players were special and my expectations have been proved to be spot-on by a six-month journey in which I have had the privilege of interviewing every single one of them for The 101 Club.

If nothing else, I have wanted their families to have a permanent reminder of why those 16 men and their manager are held in such high esteem by Town fans and illuminate the story of an extraordinary season.

But this book is not only a celebration of their exploits in 1979/80 season. It should provide an insight into what it was like to be a lower league footballer and manager in an era before Sky Sports enriched the game.

What has emerged is a series of fascinating accounts of life on and off the football field that have veered from heartbreaking to hilarious and fearful to heroic.

While former Town secretary George Binns has put Buxton's achievements into a sporting context, Huddersfield MP Barry

Sheerman has provided the social and political background with a special contribution of his own.

This labour of love also turns the spotlight on the characters behind the scenes such as legendary kit lady Nellie Thompson and groundsman Ray Chappell as well as the fan who ended up becoming an honorary member of the first-team squad.

Buxton's players achieved so much that they have also left a lasting legacy and there is no doubt in my mind that Town would not have reached the Promised Land of the Premier League had it not been for their endeavours.

I say that because there is a direct link between Buxton's team and David Wagner's heroes. That is because Town owner Dean Hoyle only chose to start watching the Terriers over their local rivals at Elland Road because of the team in blue and white stripes that was turning on the style at Leeds Road.

So when Hoyle came down to earth after the Championship play-off final and said that Buxton was responsible for the "greatest day of my life" I found myself nodding in agreement.

It was Buxton who not only lifted a football club but a whole town and showed that dreams can come true. The 101 Club will show how they did it with true Terrier Spirit.

Rob Stewart

The agony and the ecstasy

George Binns

The *Huddersfield Daily Examiner* back-page headline said it all.

There was no holding back as the normally supportive local paper poured scorn on Huddersfield Town in its sports section: 'Town Next to Bottom in Night of Shame'.

The paper's sub-editors in the old office at the bottom of Ramsden Street had had enough after a 3-1 defeat by Northampton at Leeds Road on Tuesday, September 27, 1977.

It was a game only Town's most devoted followers who made up the 3,942-strong crowd could stomach and not even Terry Gray's goal would have raised hopes of better days ahead after a defeat that stretched Town's winless start to the season to eight games.

The *Examiner's* readership had taken pride in its football club but now there was solely a feeling of embarrassment. Town had fallen to its most lowly position since the club was formed in 1908 and were second-bottom of the Football League.

"It was an ignominious fall from grace and that night was Town virtually hitting rock-bottom because we were right next to the foot of the Football League," said former Town secretary George Binns.

"There were some very dark days but they do put into perspective why Mick Buxton's team was so important. They restored pride and the 1979/80 season was the start of a resurrection after some very grim and horrible times."

In the mid-70s, Huddersfield Town, the club who had created history by winning the old Football League three times in a row in the 1920s, was a club on its knees after suffering an unprecedented slump in fortunes.

Town had begun the decade as a top-flight club and briefly led the whole Football League but then went into free-fall, tumbling from the old First Division in 1972 to the nether regions of English football thanks to three humiliating relegations in four humiliating years.

The only thing Town fans had to get excited about in the mid-70s was a concert staged at Leeds Road by chart-topping pop group Mud in June 1975.

"I've suffered for 75 years at the hands of Huddersfield Town when I've been in the depths of despair either as a supporter or employee," said Binns, from his smart bungalow in Dalton, Huddersfield.

"I've been through the full spectrum of events and emotions right from 1970 when we'd had two First Division games and were top of the pile to being next to bottom of the whole Football League.

"There were some dreadful performances. I'm sure most dyed-in-the-wool supporters, of which I've been one since 1942, wondered why they were bothering and whether we'd ever have a resurgence."

Ian Greaves had led Town into the top tier of English football in his second spell as club manager when the ever-present Frank Worthington inspired the team to the old Second Division title in 1970 with 18 goals in 42 games.

The future looked bright but things took a dramatic turn for the worse and following two successive relegations (Worthington, Trevor Cherry and Roy Ellam left after the first in 1972) Greaves resigned in June 1974 after a mid-table Third Division finish.

Celtic and Leeds United great, Bobby Collins - the first Scot to ever win the Footballer of the Year accolade - succeeded Greaves.

He was known as 'The Little General' due to his midfield combativeness but was unable to impose winning ways on players and that culminated in Fourth Division football visiting Huddersfield for the first time.

Collins jumped a sinking ship, though, in December 1975, no doubt partly in protest at compatriot and former Town manager Tom Johnston being re-hired as 'General Manager' to work with him in January the same year.

Johnston, who had masterminded two promotions at York City, flattered to deceive in his second spell as Town manager.

The club finished their first season in uncharted territory in fifth place before coach John Haselden was promoted to take over as caretaker manager in April 1977 as a ninth-placed finish beckoned.

Haselden, who would play a key role as Buxton's right-hand man, was voted into the role by the club's directors but was unable to galvanise a demoralised bunch of players.

Johnston agreed to take over for a third time but showed why there's an old adage in football that you should never go back as Town looked perfectly at home in the basement of the Football League.

"It's impossible to put a finger on one reason for the downward spiral but I do know that at boardroom level every effort was made to turn things around," Binns said.

"The directors were desperate to bring about a recovery but it's very difficult when you're on a downward spiral – as Blackpool and Portsmouth have found more recently.

"A lot of it's due to state of mind but it was hard to attract the right type of players and staff."

Johnston, who had his Town team playing in plain blue Bukta shirts in the mid-70s, should have set his sights on reversing Town's drift towards non-league football but focused on other matters.

"He came in early before everyone else, and one or twice a week he brought his shotgun and shot the local pigeons feasting on the pitch," Binns said.

"He was cute. He could sort out players and knew particularly what they would and wouldn't do.

"He was often able to forestall things they did like cutting corners on training runs and was able to stop them in their tracks."

According to Binns, Johnston was "devious, underhand yet likeable in many respects".

"He wasn't someone on whom I would turn my back. He was the kind of person who, if he were playing snooker, would cough just as his opponent was making a shot because he didn't like to lose.

"He was always smoking his pipe. When he sat next to the chairman in the directors' box, the chairman would very often get his coat burned with the little sparks from the pipe.

"He once won the Bell's manager of the month award and was handed a bottle of whisky. I had a drink that day, not because I like whisky but specifically because it was the only thing I ever got out of Tom Johnson."

Described as a 'canny Scotsman' in the club history books, he was said to be a 'shrewd strategist' whose 'quietly-spoken, pipe-smoking image hid the fact he was a stickler for discipline'.

Ironically, during Johnston's final hurrah there was a distinct lack of discipline behind the scenes at Leeds Road as Town slumped to third-bottom of the Football League after a dismal start to the 1978/79 season before Mick Buxton took over as manager.

That inauspicious start may well have been down to the fact that Johnston was in the autumn of his career and had lost the edge and energy needed to keep players on their toes and they took advantage.

"It was lax," Binns said. "Tom was getting longer in the tooth and approaching retirement age. He was stricter in his first spell. Mick Buxton had been brought in as a coach and instilled a lot of the discipline that was lacking under Tom.

"In the end, having almost reached the age of 60, he decided to retire from football (on 29 August 1978) because he could see the writing on the wall and the likelihood he'd get the sack. He took the money and ran. Perhaps it was the easy way out."

Overseeing this depressing state of affairs was Town chairman, the late Keith Longbottom, a chartered accountant whose office was opposite miners' leader Arthur Scargill's base in Barnsley.

Longbottom joined the board of directors in June 1974 and replaced Stanley Kinder as chairman days after the anguish of relegation in 1975.

"Keith was a very good man and the best chairman I worked under," Binns said.

"He was a welcome contrast to most football directors who think they know everything.

"They've been involved in businesses where they have total control and know everything from shopfloor to boardroom and don't readily take advice.

"But Keith was different and he ran the show sensibly. He quickly realised that while he knew about finances and structures of companies, he didn't understand the playing, training or coaching sides of football.

"He was astute enough to know which members of his staff he could 100 per cent rely upon. He confided in them, took notice of them and ran the club with their opinions in mind.

"That's why there was guarded optimism when Mick Buxton was appointed manager and he even trusted him so much he sanctioned a £40,000 transfer fee to bring Steve Kindon to Huddersfield from Burnley. It was a lot of money but it paid off."

Being a director was clearly not a role for the thin-skinned, judging by Longbottom's comments. "I had many happy times with promotion but also very traumatic times following relegation. Being a Huddersfield Town director can be a very dangerous thing to be.

"Cars damaged, threatening phone calls at home and not simply for me but my family too. Being Huddersfield born-and-bred, it was very difficult to throw in the towel. All in all, over the years it was a rewarding time."

Binns is not one to readily give away secrets but it would seem Longbottom was no typical club supremo.

"Mostly, their hearts were in the right place but they were, nevertheless, loveable rogues and I was too honest when dealing with them," Binns said.

"As a club we were too honourable and you know what I'm talking about without me saying anything.

"It was the illegal signing of players and that sort of thing. I could tell you which managers wanted backhanders but I'd best not.

"There were a lot of things done via companies either owned or associated with directors.

"That was one of the main things but there was all sorts of stuff going on. Their morals were not what they should have been."

Through thick and thin, Binns kept in order as Town's main

administrator from the day he started working for the club full-time as assistant secretary in 1969 before becoming secretary in 1974.

He held that role until 1991 when he was asked by Town's board of directors to quit his role and lead the team which would build what is now the John Smith's Stadium, as stadium development administrator.

"By modern-day standards Leeds Road was a pit," Binns said. "There were dingy corridors and toilets which were terrible but that was common. It was a throwback to the 1930s and what replaced it was a breathtaking and award-winning building."

Binns began supporting Town in the wartime league era when an array of internationals adorned the club such as Manchester City goalkeeper Frank Swift because footballers had to turn out for the club closest to their barracks.

After learning his trade with a chartered accountancy in Huddersfield, there were two years' national service for Binns and a spell in the textile industry before he responded to Town's calling.

"It was back in 1967 when I started on match days, helping out a friend (Bill Brook) who was the club's first commercial executive and wanted someone he could trust to handle money.

"I eventually took the club secretary's job and to this day, I've never known why but I did. It's been my passion – not simply a job.

"Literally every aspect of club affairs aside from dealing with the players themselves in relation to training and playing of matches was my responsibility.

"Football clubs didn't have the infrastructure that they do now. You had five or six people who did everything on a financial shoestring.

"I dealt with all administration, board meeting minutes, transfers, buying for the club shop. I made arrangements for games and sorted out travel for away games."

"I even ended up as editor of the matchday programme. Everything in it cost next to nothing. We'd get friendly hacks to contribute and charge very little."

It was several jobs rolled into one but multi-tasking was not reflected in his wage packet.

"I didn't receive a king's ransom. At first, I got £1,500-a-year which went up to about £40 a week while the players were earning about £60-65 a week.

"I was never particularly bothered about what I got paid. I just enjoyed my job, dealing with all the problems, stewards, policing and coping with everything that occurred."

It was his job to make sure things ran smoothly on match days but even the best-laid plans can fail, as they did when Town lost 3-1 to Portsmouth on October 13, 1979.

"We'd had a tremendous start to the season and I was expecting a crowd of about 5-6,000. We were going great guns but still how could I have anticipated the crowd of about 16,000 that was three times the average gate.

"We had plenty of turnstiles so the facilities were there but we didn't have the necessary manpower. I'd plan for double the expected crowd but never treble so we had long queues.

"Of course, we should have known better. At least that's what supporters said. 'You'd won six or seven games in a row so you should have realised we were going to see you.'

"We ran out of programmes before kick off and people were up in arms. It was the same with tea and coffee, Bovril and meat pies. I hate to think what the queue for the toilets was like. Maybe if we'd won no one would have cared."

Binns was always in the firing line – even at home.

"Whatever happened on the day of a game, win, lose or draw, there were always grumbles.

"They'd come to see me after a game or make contact over the telephone because my number was in the book so I'd get calls on Saturday night and Sunday.

"I'd stay late on Monday so they could see me after work but three-quarters of them never turned up. With those who did, once we went through the six-week planning process, they would change their views."

It was an exception to the rule but Binns receive no complaints whatsoever on that giddy day in May 1979 when the Fourth Division title was won.

"The darkest of dark days weren't too far behind us but the day we beat Hartlepool was just the opposite - it was joy untold.

"Everything about that day was super apart from our abysmal first-half performance.

"There was even drama off the field for the Football League who had one of their management board stationed equidistant between Huddersfield and our title rivals in Walsall.

"He had instructions to deliver the trophy to the right address once he knew which way the wind was blowing. Fortunately, we equalised after half-time, he gambled, headed to Huddersfield and the silverware was handed over immediately after the game."

Binns found himself right in the thick of the celebrations.

"That evening was the height of elation and it was the last time I was ever the worse for wear due to alcohol.

"We had Champagne put on ice and it flowed freely. It was only the second time in my life I'd ever been anywhere near what you could describe as drunk.

"We'd celebrated so much that I was very, very happy by seven o'clock, when I decided I had to go home and get changed for the celebratory banquet that evening (at the Greenhead Masonic Hall).

"I wasn't blind-drunk but I'd been a little bit worse for wear and I dropped the trophy.

"It ran down a slope into the car park. It ended up tucked safely under my bed that night but if it's still got a bit of a dent in it then I have to confess it's my fault."

....

The bespectacled George Binns would appear to be unlikely adversary for the hooligans who blighted English football but he still took them all on with a little help from Big Brother.

"I was instrumental in trying to sort out hooliganism in the early 80s

when Leeds United came to Leeds Road and their fans were at the height of their powers in terms of hooliganism.

"We knew they were going to wreck the ground as best they could and we, myself and the senior policeman of that day, George Callaghan, decided we'd use high-quality colour hand-held cameras for the first time.

"They'd not been used in football at that time, except for some very poor quality black and white ones that were designed for police control to direct officers to where there were problems.

"We decided we'd use the cameras to get close-ups to identify people who were causing the problems to bring wrong-doers to justice.

"As expected the Leeds fans ran riot and they tried to wreck the place from start to finish thinking they were immune but they were wrong.

"Cameras had never been used as evidence in a court of law but we got the first conviction based on that particular game."

But Binns wasn't finished there as he helped tackle the scourge of the modern-day game.

"I met at the Farnley Cock pub with George Callaghan and Lord Faulkner of Worcester, for the Government, to discuss what we'd done and we decided that was the way forward to sort out hooliganism.

"It was so successful that the then Prime Minister, Margaret Thatcher, asked us to do a presentation at 10 Downing Street and then instructed that all football clubs should have permanent, high-quality cameras.

"We were going to be the first club to install them but right at the last-minute there was a high-profile game at Anfield and they asked if Liverpool could have the ones we'd ordered.

"It meant we were denied another little place in history but it changed the pattern of the way things were for the better."

Moonshadow

Peter Hart

'It was the best of times, it was the worst of times, it was the age of wisdom, it was the age of foolishness, it was the epoch of belief, it was the epoch of incredulity, it was the season of light, it was the season of darkness, it was the spring of hope, it was the winter of despair.'

Most Town fans who studied O-level English back in their secondary schooldays – like your author at Moor End High School - will recognise these are the words of Charles Dickens from A Tale of Two Cities rather than a former Town player's thoughts.

But these extraordinary words have been chosen because they perfectly reflect the topsy-turvy journey that former Town skipper Peter Hart embarked upon after leaving school and ended with him lifting the Fourth Division trophy at the age of just 22.

"There were two parallels lines in the 1970s, which were my personal experience of Huddersfield, which was wonderful, and the club's demise, which was awful," said Hart. "In spite of the fact the club was plummeting, it was such an exciting time for me."

The 60-year-old Hart, who is now the Vicar of Cannock and Huntington as well as being Walsall Football Club's chaplain, was reflecting on his mixed emotions in the office of the vicarage which is his base in the West Midlands.

"It's strange but they were the happiest football days of my life. Despite the decline, despite the rot, Huddersfield was such an important part of my life. It was great place to be in spite of the fact it was the worst period of the club's existence.

"Forgive the language when I say it was only the Fourth Division title but it was way more than that. The 70s was a decade most would want to forget but 1980 was a watershed.

"It was turning point from demise to beginning of some sort of success. Although it's taken 30-odd years for Town to get back to the top division, it did at least stop the rot."

Hart had put his signature on the dotted line for Huddersfield Town on his 15th birthday – August 14, 1971 – after Mexborough Grammar School's headmaster allowed him to leave education a year earlier than his peers to try to carve himself a career in football.

"Growing up as a working-class lad in Mexborough (South Yorkshire) there wasn't a lot to do. You had to make your own entertainment and for me it was picking up a football and going down to the park and playing games with the other kids.

"Having fallen in love with football, I threw away my grammar school education. I can't remember doing anything after the first year because football loomed large over everything else. It was an opportunity to make something of myself because I wasn't going to do anything academically."

His commitment paid dividends as an envelope dropped through the letterbox at the council-owned maisonette the Harts called home ("We didn't have a phone so that was the only way to get in touch.") inviting him for a trial.

"We had a evening game under floodlights which were really remarkable and just so impressive.

"There were two teams of triallists, one in blue and white stripes and the other in red and back stripes. I even remember the music prior to the game. We were warming up to the Cat Stevens song 'I'm bein' followed by a Moonshadow'.

"It was a big club and big ground so it was very exciting. I played in midfield but I clearly didn't have enough technical ability to go on and establish myself there. Thankfully, they saw enough in me to think I had what it took to be a professional.

"So I signed schoolboy forms which committed you to a club in those days. It was designed to stop you upping sticks and trying your luck elsewhere if you fancied a different club in case anything else came up.

"I was happy with that arrangement. Having been to Huddersfield and become smitten by the club I would not have gone anywhere else. I was invited to go to Sheffield United and there were rumours about other clubs but I was committed to Huddersfield.

"It might sound daft but 'Field of Dreams' would be a pretty apt way to describe the Leeds Road ground in those days when we were in the First Division with Frank Worthington, Roy Ellam and Trevor Cherry."

Still, as an apprentice, Hart had to do his bit to make sure the Leeds Road facilities were fit for established professional footballers with a set of menial tasks, aimed at keeping the place spick and span.

"My responsibility was the second team bath and showers and that extended to do the medical room, washing room, drying room, cleaning toilets and keeping the passageway tidy but nothing, absolutely nothing, would dampen my enthusiasm."

He was paid £6.47-a-week after National Insurance and had his accommodation – or digs as they were known - paid for along with a dozen other apprentices in a house in Fixby overseen by someone he reverentially refers to as Mrs Jones.

"Between 15 and 17 all we wanted to do was become footballers so we stayed on the straight and narrow

"Surely there must have been things as I look back now – as a 60-year-old man - that I wouldn't do now but I can't look back and say I have regrets because I don't.

"Everyone wanted to earn a living but most players in those days would have played for nothing because that's all they wanted to do.

"I don't know whether or not the club took advantage but the fact is that the power lay with paymasters, not players.

"The Bosman ruling on freedom of movement changed all that. It meant players had power over their own destiny.

"Once a contract expires you're free. That's good if you're a decent player but not necessarily that good if you're clinging on."

That was anything but the case for Hart and his fellow teenagers as they secured Town a place in the FA Youth Cup Final for the first time in 1974 when the side he captained narrowly lost over two legs to Tottenham.

The first game at White Hart Lane ended in a 1-1 draw after Town striker Bob Newton cancelled out John Margerrison's goal before a season-high 15,300 fans saw Spurs' Roger Gibbins settle the contest in extra-time at Leeds Road.

Hart also had plenty to shout about when Town jetted off to a youth tournament in Portugal. It was the first time Hart and most of his colleagues had flown and they won the competition after beating Benfica 3-0 on penalties in the final and consequently had wages bumped up to £28 a week.

"It was the most remarkable time because leaving school and becoming a footballer was exciting in itself but also we had a really good youth team and good bunch of apprentices like Bob Newton, Dick Taylor and Martin Fowler as well as Francis Firth and Lloyd Maitland.

"We were all lucky because the manager, Ian Greaves, gave young players the opportunity to prove themselves for the reserves in the Central League against the likes of Liverpool, Everton, Manchester City, Manchester United and Leeds.

"You could find yourself up against internationals coming back from injury. I played against stars like Joe Royle, Brian Kidd, Tommy Smith and Steve Heighway. For a 15-year old playing in the Central League against that calibre of player convinced you everything was potentially up for grabs."

At the age of 16, Hart also had to deal with the biggest personal setback of his life when he lost his dad, a train driver. He died at the age of 55 due to coronary heart disease some six months before his son's Town debut. (Hart himself recently underwent surgery after having a heart attack.)

"Ian Greaves was incredibly gentle and compassionate, despite being a big, strong man, so I always had a huge regard for him.

"He was a great man who was there when I really needed him. He was very positive about the youth team. He encouraged and inspired. I just wish I could have talked to him a lot more after he'd left.

"I once skipped training and put it down to having flu. 'Flu? Flu?, I'll give you flu.....I got a right rollicking. I never skipped training again."

Making up for lost time, Hart wrote his way into Town's history books by becoming the youngest ever player to figure in a first-team game. That was at the tender age of 16 years and 229 days when he stepped out to face Southend United on May 30, 1974, in front of 4,453 supporters.

"Roy Ellam sent me a telegram wishing me all the best. I was centre-half and up against Chris Guthrie who was a big strong lad, not a bruiser but a good old–fashioned striker. We lost 1-0 which spoiled things."

He had to bide his team before a regular first-team slot was secured but still managed to get his first car – a second-hand, four-year-old Ford Cortina – while he worked his way up the ranks.

"I can't remember where I got it from but I do know where it went because I wrote it off on the day of a game and it ended up in the scrapyard.

"I was driving down Leeds Road when a Land Rover pulled out and I smashed into it.

"The Land Rover sped away and my car was written off. It was all a bit of a shock but I wasn't hurt and so I played that night against Tranmere Rovers and did all right."

He would also get married in 1978 at the age of 20, to Liz, who is the mother of his two daughters. They met while she was serving drinks at Johnny's nightclub in Huddersfield where Town players unwound after midweek matches.

More often than not Hart's colleagues would have been drowning sorrows as Town hurtled towards the bottom of the Football League and attendances plummeted with locals turning their back on his team.

Just 1,638 people turned up to watch Town play Bournemouth in an end-of-season game in April 29, 1978. That has gone down in history as the lowest league crowd in the club's history, when gates at wartime games, like the visit of York City in January 1940, which attracted just only 332 people, are disregarded.

"It was an arena that had been capable of holding 67,000 (a record 67,057 saw Town host Arsenal in the FA Cup sixth round in February 1932) when the club was in its pomp so playing in front of such small crowds was dreadful. But that was tangible, real-life evidence of demise. The club had fallen a huge distance. It had fallen from grace."

Greaves, Bobby Collins and Tom Johnston – who made Hart the Town captain - all tried and failed to resuscitate the ailing club.

"Things had already been sinking when Tom came back when we were in the Third Division. He didn't so much as encourage the decline, he simply came when the decline was in progress and he wasn't able to turn it around.

"It might have been to do with the fact that he was slightly more relaxed and easy-going and maybe what it needed was a manager who could change the tone of the club.

"It was going downhill but I was only interested in playing, not the politics of the club, so I can't explain why it went wrong. But once momentum takes hold it's difficult to arrest and there was clearly a negative momentum."

Hart saw noticeable improvement once Buxton picked up the poisoned chalice.

"Our downward spiral was only broken when Mick Buxton took the club by the scruff of the neck. Things had fallen into disarray but, by-gum, he took control.

"All the dynamics of his relationships with us players changed as he went from being a coach to being the boss.

"I remember once asking him what should we call him because prior to that he'd been a coach. There was no hesitation. 'Boss,' he said.

"That term of address was fine with me because respect is a big thing in football. It was part of the reason he was a success.

"I know calling someone boss doesn't necessarily mean you respect them but besides being called boss he earned that respect.

"And at times he could be fearsome, too. If you stepped out of line then he'd let you know but overall he was a damned good manager."

Despite Buxton's appointment, apathy still reigned around the area and just 1,680 watched a 1-1 draw against Torquay in April 30, 1979, but seeds of success had been sown.

"Mick was a very positive force. He energised the club. He knew what he wanted and where he wanted to go. If you didn't want to go there with him then that was tough because he was in charge.

"He wanted to play in a certain style. He liked to press high up the pitch and liked his team to work hard and clearly got the best out of a bunch of players who had previously not done that well."

Hart was switched from right-back to central midfield by Buxton.

"My job was to get stuck in, win the ball and pass it. There wasn't always a great deal of flair and skill but there was endeavor and lots of aggression from myself.

"You get to know your limitations and I settled into my role as a defensive midfielder. Stopping the opposition from playing was my strength. Mick Laverick passed the ball well so we complemented each other nicely in central midfield.

"I also chipped in with a few goals. I scored five in that (1979/80) season in the first nine matches which was unusual. I got a couple against Port Vale when the rest of the division stood up and took notice of us (it was Town's biggest win since an 8-2 win over Everton in April 1953) and I scored a cracker against Stockport.

"But one of my stand-out moments was the own goal I scored at Hereford which was a wonderful effort. Our goalie had come out to the edge of his box and when I attempted to pass the ball back it sailed over him."

Hart was clearly Buxton's team in microcosm and Town nipped ahead of Walsall on the finishing line.

"There was no captain's armband but I always tried to lead by example. I had a never-say-die attitude and you kept going till the final whistle.

"As a team we embodied Mick Buxton because we were hard-working, committed and aggressive and we liked to attack, get players forward and score goals.

"Walsall were a lot more of a football team. They had some really quality, flair players, like player-manager Alan Buckley who was outstanding.

"They were not as well organised as us so there was a contrast but that contrast was both positive and good.

"We were very much on a par. We could play football but even though our way was a more disciplined approach that ought not to undermine what a good team we were."

Both games against Walsall were drawn 1-1 but the Saddlers had their noses in front as the run-in unfolded.

"Mick's strength of character and determination meant there was no slacking and that epitomised the difference between the two sides.

"By Easter they'd got promoted and then faded but, due to Mick's force of character, there was no way we'd fade because we were set out to give everything right until the end of every match."

That was the case right until the season's and Hart's finale when Hartlepool visited Leeds Road on May 3, 1980.

Hart, who played a key role in the winning goal against Hartlepool, had played 229 times for Town and scored eight goals before a £70,000 move to Walsall the following August.

"I didn't leave for money but I left as a matter of principle. I felt loyalty should be rewarded but a lot more money was being offered to attract new players to the club

"Now I'm older and wiser I realise that's the way the game works. Had I been as wise then I might've just taken what was on offer, stayed put and got on with it.

"I do regret leaving when I did because it was my club but I allowed emotions to sway me. I ended up cutting my nose off to spite my face."

....

Peter Hart appears to be living proof that God acts in mysterious ways – although he denies that is the case.

He has made a journey from the Town midfield trenches to the church pulpit but he is swift to challenge the notion two are incompatible.

"Some people may reckon that being a vicar is at odds with being

an aggressive, gritty footballer but I don't think that's the case.

"As a player, I was always very honest, always fully committed to the team and the cause and always passionate. Surely those are qualities that can be equated with Christian faith."

Hart trained to become a vicar after hanging up his boots at Walsall but first found God after the birth of his second daughter while at the peak of his football powers with the Saddlers.

"I was a tough player, an uncompromising one but I don't think I was never dirty. I never wanted to deliberately harm anyone.

"Football taught me a lot. You have to think about focus, teamwork; being determined particularly when things do not go well.

"I'm very positive about the way sport and my faith come together. It teaches you a heck of a lot about life, how to handle emotions and remain focused."

From Russia with love

by Huddersfield MP Barry Sheerman

I first became aware of the tremendous passion that Huddersfield Town commands thanks to our former Prime Minister Harold Wilson.

That was in 1979 when I had the honour of being joined on the General Election campaign trail by the greatest of Town fans.

Sadly, his brain was deteriorating – he'd had to stand down as PM in 1976 – but his wife Mary allowed him to spend a day with me, which is something I fondly remember.

It quickly became apparent just how much Town meant to him because he kept on producing what must have been one of his prized possessions – a 1923/24 Huddersfield Town cigarette card.

"Look at this card and look on the back," he said. "I was in Moscow and I showed it to Leonid Brezhnev (the former leader of the Soviet Union) and he thought I wanted his autograph and look he's signed it on the back for me."

It made us both laugh and it still brings a smile to my face. It's also a reminder of just how fiercely proud he was of his local football club. Harold epitomised the tremendous passion there is for Huddersfield Town and I really enjoyed accompanying him to watch Town play.

People look fondly at our greatest days when the club ruled the football world under Herbert Chapman. We always kept faith that one day we would come back to the top again and here we are.

While our passion for Town has been an enduring feature of local life, the social and political landscape has transformed since I was first elected as a Labour MP.

The period between 1979 and 1980 was a watershed for the town. Huddersfield went from being a very traditional Yorkshire town to one that was planning for the future. You could see the town changing rapidly as jobs in manufacturing declined and were replaced by jobs in the service sector.

For over 150 years Huddersfield had been a prime manufacturing town, famous for textiles, engineering and chemicals. At its peak, 6,000 people worked at the ICI plant on Leeds Road. Today there's a workforce of about 500 and only 10 per cent of people manufacture anything in the town. Like the rest of the country, 60 per cent work in private services and 30 per cent of us now work in public services like education and health.

When I first became an MP, the polytechnic (as the University of Huddersfield was known then) was tiny compared to what is now a very big, thriving seat of education and our town's biggest employer.

In 1979, we'd just come through that 'Winter of Discontent' under the then Prime Minister Jim Callaghan. Industrial strife was high and people were very resentful about the state of the economy.

People in Liverpool weren't being buried and piles of rubbish were littering the streets of London. It was an unhappy time for a lot of people, and this was followed by the 1983/84 miners' strike.

Although times were tough, Huddersfield still had a diverse local economy and the capacity to adapt to change, which meant that we survived better than many other towns.

Back in 1979, social life was much more traditional and at the heart of the social life would be watching Town playing football or Fartown rugby league. You just needed to look at the *Huddersfield Daily Examiner* coverage to see how much those clubs meant to our community.

However, Fartown's home was very ramshackle and, while Town's Leeds Road ground was loved, it was hardly fit for purpose in the modern age.

In 1980, I started something called 'Huddersfield 2000' with some leading local champions. Chaired by ICI's MD, Brian Smith, Huddersfield 2000 was set up to look to the future of our town over the long term. We commissioned a report from Habitat founder Sir Terence Conran's consultancy, which told us we needed to re-discover the excellence Huddersfield was synonymous with in areas like textiles and engineering.

Out of that report emerged the need for a new centre for sport and we managed to persuade ICI to give us the large piece of land where the John Smith's Stadium is located for a pound. That's why I've always jokingly said don't dig too deep under the pitch because there may be a lot of chemicals underneath!

At the time I was fighting for Fartown as they hadn't paid any PAYE for about five years and Inland Revenue were after them. Huddersfield Town weren't much better off.

So the two clubs were in dark days and they were persuaded that going to a new shared stadium was the best route to a prosperous future.

The brilliance of the plan was that it wasn't a PFI (Public Finance Initiative) but a Public-Private Partnership – 30 per cent for each club and 40 per cent for the council. Other football clubs then copied this model. For example, Bolton attracted Paul Fletcher who had masterminded the stadium development. That was the greatest form of flattery. However, they did not poach our brilliant John Harman, the pioneering leader of the local council.

Huddersfield's dynamism and ability to look to the future is symbolised by the replacement of Leeds Road and Fartown with John Smith's Stadium. People can now enjoy watching high-quality sport in a wonderful stadium. We're also moving forward with the HD1 development, so things are looking good on and off the football field.

I had a young family in those days when Mick Buxton was leading Town's renaissance in the 1980s and if I'd spent my Saturday afternoons watching Town I'd have ended up in the divorce courts. But I did go to as many games as I could.

You need a bit luck in football and I think Town have been doubly fortunate because of the coincidence of Dean Hoyle and David Wagner. We were crying out for a fantastic and solid owner, which we've got with Dean who's devoted to the club. His masterstroke was appointing a really brilliant manager and that's what David has been. Long may he stay and allow us to rule in the Premier League. As long as we retain them my hopes are high.

Snookered

Mick Buxton

There was an immaculate snooker table beneath the wooden stand at the old Leeds Road ground that by all accounts would keep Town players entertained for hours on end.

The lure of green baize beneath the main stand proved so attractive that there was barely time for a frame after Mick Buxton took over the managerial reins from Tom Johnston.

Buxton ordered its immediate removal as he laid down the law to players more interested in working on their potting skills with a frame or two than developing passing skills down at Leeds Road playing fields.

"The first thing I had to do was to get rid of the club's snooker table," said Buxton as he sipped on a tea in the armchair at the pristine Barnsley bungalow that he and wife Maureen call home.

"The snooker table had to go because the quickest most of the players ran was when training finished and they wanted to be first back to get on that ruddy thing.

"They seemed to be more interested in playing snooker than going out ruddy training. So we stopped all that. The people at the club couldn't believe it when there was no snooker table there.

"But it had to be done. It ended up getting sold by the club but I didn't care where it went or where the money had gone as long as it was out of their sight so they could focus on their jobs.

"The players were stunned but I couldn't give a monkey's what they thought. Their thoughts on the matter didn't bother me in the slightest."

Buxton, who was just 36 when Town won the Fourth Division title, was wasting no time in restoring order after Johnston had retired and he took charge on a caretaker basis.

"The players had no respect. They didn't respect the management, they didn't respect the staff, they didn't respect each other, they didn't respect the facilities and, worst of all, they didn't respect Huddersfield Town Football Club.

"There was one incident when the players trooped through the manager's car in their dirty training gear which was absolutely diabolical. If they'd done that with me, they'd have been straight out the door."

There was method in Buxton's madness over the state of play behind the scenes.

"I never looked at it as stamping my authority on the club – it was just how things should be done.

"I knew exactly what I wanted to do and what sort of team I wanted to put together. I wanted players to be very disciplined; to be professionals.

"There were lines drawn in the sand sharpish because I like things to be nice and tidy and I made things nice and smart. It was simple as that.

"We had the whole place cleaned up. Everything was scrubbed up every day, the dressing rooms, the corridors, so you came into a good environment.

"But you had to look after that environment because you were part of it. That was where the discipline first starts. If you haven't got that you haven't got a prayer.

"They would come in and kick balls all over the place so there were dirty ball marks on all the walls.

"It riled me that so I stopped all of that and it meant that when they came back from training, stuff wasn't just thrown on the floor.

"We had Nellie (Thompson) who did all the washing. She was a wonderful part of the club and I asked the lads: 'Why should she have to come in and pick up all your bloody dirty gear?' I wasn't having it.

"Everybody had to clean their own boots. It's part of the trade. If you're a tradesman you look after your gear and footballers should be no different. If boots weren't clean you'd be in trouble."

That emphasis on discipline could be put down to his upbringing in the mining community of Ryhope in the North East of England – where his mum is still going strong well into her 90s.

It was also down to a football education which saw him play for Sunderland and Durham boys before leaving school and home at the age of 15 and heading across the Pennines to Burnley, when the Lancashire club was at its peak.

"I was very fortunate. There was a playing staff of 50 and about 35 came from the North East. They were very much into coaching at Burnley, particularly working on skills, controlling a ball, passing a ball, movement off the ball.

"It was wonderful. The club had a terrific practice ground and an indoor training area. You didn't have to go begging, borrowing and stealing a piece of ground to work on which is what I had to do at Huddersfield when I first started.

"I picked up a lot of good points from those Burnley days because there was such a good ethos. I knew exactly what I wanted to do, how I wanted to do it and what team I wanted to put together."

Buxton, figured 16 times for Burnley in the First Division but his playing career was cut short by injury when he was on Halifax's books. He got stuck into coaching at Watford, Mansfield and then Southend before he began to work at Leeds Road as first-team coach on December 13, 1977.

"A lot of hard work had been put in at Southend and Dave Smith and I were just starting to reap the benefits," Buxton told *Huddersfield Daily Examiner* reporter Paul Clark after he re-located. "But if your family isn't enjoying life it is impossible to concentrate on your job properly. Regardless of anything, family comes first."

He went back over his reasoning at his Barnsley home with its panoramic views of Yorkshire countryside.

"The reason I became a coach at Huddersfield is because we just got fed up living in Southend.

"There was nothing wrong with the club and the manager, Dave Smith, was a good friend of mine.

"We still had our house in Barnsley and preferred to be back up North. We wanted a stable place for our two lads who'd been like gypsies with all the moving around."

"I went in and told Dave from this moment onwards I'm finished. He couldn't believe it but I just told him I needed to get back to Barnsley. I ended up on the dole queue so I needed to find a job quickly."

Buxton had heard about a vacancy arising at Town when his former colleague, the late Walter Joyce, moved to Rochdale, so he was straight on the phone to Town manager Johnston "to see if there were any jobs going".

"I was coming to watch a Town game and I stopped on the A1 just outside Cambridge and spoke to Tom. I'd never met him in my life but it was a matter of taking the bull by the horns when you haven't got a job and that was it."

Buxton was no right-hand man because "Tom didn't believe in that sort of thing" so he was the first team coach with John Haselden looking after reserves.

The contrasts between Johnston and Buxton quickly became apparent on the training ground.

"Tom's ideas of coaching footballers were totally different to mine but you had to go along with what Tom said.

"Normally you know well in advance what you are going to be doing so you can plan what you want to do.

"Tom would come in in the morning, reading the papers and smoking his pipe and then he'd say: 'Right I think we'll do a bit of passing today.'

"There's a hell of a lot you can do with a bit of passing. So in other words there was nothing planned.

"It was off the top of your head. You'd have to go out and do something and then he could very well interrupt and spoil it all.

"It was very frustrating. In fairness to Tom, he had success at York City where he got promotion. But he was a different era to me.

"With me everything was organised. We knew what we wanted to do on any given day and for any particular session.

"It was difficult because Tom was a pretty old guy, I was a pretty young guy and his ideas to running a club were totally different to mine. I respected his ideas but that sort of situation always makes life difficult."

Those were the days that Town practiced on the council-owned Leeds Road Playing Fields, a triangular strip of land down in vast Huddersfield's industrial corridor.

It was sandwiched between the canal on one side and the giant ICI chemical complex and was home to every standard of local football as well as local cricket matches with Birkby Old Boys calling it home.

"The facilities were awful although the council groundsman did well for us by finding us a bit of grass to work on.

"We bought portable goals, which we kept down there and the lads had to cart them to whichever part of the ground we'd been told we could use.

"Most days we ran down there and back alongside the canal towpath and if it happened to be your birthday then it was unlucky because you'd get thrown in the canal.

"No one was spared. Not even big Sam Allardyce. I was the only person in all my time at Huddersfield not to get thrown in the canal because my birthday was in between the seasons."

His players would become familiar with Kilner Bank, especially during pre-season for hill running sessions. He also had them training two afternoons a week, which didn't go down well.

"It wasn't a case of finish at 12 and then off you go. The buses sometimes had their lights on when they came back.

"But I wasn't doing that because I had nothing better to do. Far from it. It was so we could get fitter, work on skills and then develop moves and set-pieces.

"I told them straight. 'We're not a playschool. You don't turn up here for us to keep you happy. This is your place of work.' People have to dig holes in the road. They don't like to do it but they've got to do it."

"I was straight with them. 'You're very fortunate that you do something you want to do. You want to run around, you want to kick a ball about. So when you come here you will be disciplined enough to do your job properly. You turn up on time and then when we train you work hard. We're not here to have a laugh and a joke.'

Buxton did not see eye-to-eye with popular winger Kevin Johnson.

"He was a favourite with the fans but, for me, he was a waste of space - a tricky devil when he got the ball but a horrible bugger. He wasn't my cup of tea.

"He was well liked by the fans and quite few people said 'I bet you wish you had Kevin Johnson' but he wouldn't have lasted very long.

"Once he kicked a bollard, probably in frustration at me. I told him to put it back twice. They were all stood there.

"I told him 'you ain't buggering around with someone now. You're going to do what I'm telling you to do. Get that and put it back.'

"I told him to take his time because I had all day but you'll put that bollard back. It was five o'clock."

Buxton won the battle of wills and Johnson moved on to Halifax in 1978.

"Players will murder you if you don't keep on top of them all the time. They will play on you and they will take you to the cleaners.

"You've always got to be watching them and how they tick. I've seen players kid the fitness people to death and they think they'd better stop. But they're never really tired.

"If my players complained to me that they were tired, I'd say 'okay, let's do it again to make sure you're not tired and they'd run like hell.""

Buxton took over the reins on a caretaker basis when Johnston announced his retirement.

"We were third-bottom when I took over but it was diabolical that a club of Huddersfield Town's stature should be in the nether regions of the Football League.

"The season hadn't started very well and come September after a few games – we'd lost at Scunthorpe in a Friday night game – the following morning (chairman) Keith Longbottom got in touch telling me Tom was going and asking if I'd like to take over.

"It seemed like I'd be caretaker manager while they kept their options open but at the same time I thought it's up to me to prove

I can do this job and off we went.

"I honestly believed it was a job I could do. I had great belief in my ability. We were down near the foot of the table for a reason.

"It was just a matter of putting a few things right. I knew we wouldn't go down. Even with bad players if you get them organised and get them working and playing to their strengths you'll move up.

"I saw Dave Sutton trying to chip ball across penalty box. 'Who you think you are? Franz Beckenbauer?' I told him if he ever did that again he'd never play for the club again."

He then turned his mind to wider tactical matters but would be handed the job on a permanent basis at the end of October.

"I was very strong on fitness so the players worked harder than they'd ever worked. I'd missed pre-season but I made up for it the following summer."

"I wanted to shape the team so it was attacking but sound defensively to avoid conceding stupid goals and stop having to play catch-up so we worked a lot defensively and then on how we'd spring into attack."

"We had to go back to basics and the basics were that we had players who wanted to work and who wanted to improve and wanted to play for the club."

....

Mick Buxton is proud of his record of developing young players during his days as Town manager.

He may have brought in players who became Town legends like Steve Kindon, Ian Robins and Brian Stanton but he also nurtured up-and-coming talent like Mark Lillis and many more young footballers.

"It was something that I really enjoyed and really believed in," said Buxton.

"People don't really comment on the players that we produced in our days at Huddersfield Town but about 20 of them went on to have

really, really good careers.

"We took a lot of kids from school and they really prospered at Leeds Road. I'm thinking of the likes of Peter Valentine, Simon Trevitt and Graham Mitchell and Liam Robinson.

"Then there's Peter Butler and Liam Measham as well plus Julian Winter and Andy Watson who went on to be Town's chief executives. I could go on forever."

Buxton also had spells in charge at Sunderland and Scunthorpe and his track record was so impressive that he was handed a job with the Premier League to develop its academy system.

"I'd finished managing and to be perfectly honest I'd had enough of it; I didn't particularly want to work as a manager anymore," said Buxton.

"Then John Barnwell, who was chairman of the Professional Footballers' Association, put me in touch with people and I got the job with the Premier League which I did for 12 years until I retired a few years ago."

Dave Richardson was in overall charge of improving the academy system with former Sunderland manager Len Ashurst looking after clubs in the South and Buxton patrolling the North with three office staff providing support.

"It was a job that I thoroughly enjoyed," Buxton said. "I remember seeing little Fabian Delph playing for Bradford City Under-10s against Notts County when Steve Smith was in charge of their youth set-up.

"I remember seeing Ross Barklay playing for Everton one Tuesday afternoon at Newcastle against their Under-18s and I told Ray Hall who was in charge of Everton I liked the right-back. 'Aye, he's good and he's only 15 years old.' You could see then he was a really talented player. The same applied to Wayne Rooney who I saw when he was playing for Everton's Under-13s.

"One player that really catches my eye these days is Marcus Rashford. He's not only fast and skilful but he's so powerful that no one can knock him over. He's the best player England have got."

A bum note

Alan Starling

Mick Buxton shoved an official-looking letter across the desk in the Huddersfield Town manager's office in the direction of his goalkeeper Alan Starling.

It was correspondence from Humberside Police and it stated that Starling was in trouble for his antics when he dropped his shorts during Town's visit to Scunthorpe United's former home, The Old Showground.

Starling had his collar felt by the long arm of the law for being unable to ignore the chorus of 'Starling, Starling, show us your arse' that became a favourite chant amongst Town fans in the Cowshed and on away trips.

"There used to be stick-on eyes that you could get from joke shops and, well, I used to have a pair that I would stick on each cheek of my buttocks," Starling said.

"And when the fans used to sing their chorus of 'Starling, Starling, show us your arse,' the shorts would come down and the eyes were there.

"I used to do it on a regular basis to give the fans a laugh but I ended up getting done for doing a moony by the police after a game at Scunthorpe.

"A female constable stationed behind the goal saw what I did and told me in no uncertain terms, not to do it again.

"I honestly thought she was just mucking about but I did it again and thought nothing of it.

"But then I got called into the office by Mick on Monday morning and he told me the police had done me for bearing my buttocks and fined me the princely sum of £50.

"That was just the sort of thing you got up to in those days. Thankfully, I think Mick might have just seen the funny side of it.

"That was probably because it was just after the Arsenal defender Sammy Nelson had been fined £500 by the FA of showing his backside at Highbury. Mick reckoned I was very fortunate to escape with a £50 fine."

Buxton's forgiving attitude may have been down to the goalkeeping prowess displayed by Starling at Scunthorpe.

According to the *Huddersfield Daily Examiner's* Town reporter Paul Clark, Starling had 'produced a spell-binding one-handed save that provoked some observers to compare it with the magical moment Gordon Banks conjured up against Pele in the 1970 World Cup.'

It was on his way down the M5 for a game of golf at Celtic Manor in South Wales, that Starling also recalled endearing himself to supporters by having a crafty cigarette during matches.

"People of a certain vintage will remember that here used to be stick-on ashtrays that people used to put in their cars.

"I used to have one that I would stick down my shorts and put on one of my goalposts but I made sure it was only our supporters that could see the ashtray.

"There was a time when we were playing up at Darlington at the old Feethams ground and our supporters were behind my goal and I was caught out having a crafty cigarette during the match.

"They were very kind to me. They would light a cigarette and if the ball was up the other end of the field, they would hand it to me and I'd have a couple of puffs. You wouldn't get that happening now with TV cameras and smartphones all over the place at football grounds."

Nor would you get Starling – who let fans take penalties against him as he warmed up for away games - and his team-mates pulling out of training to go and play snooker before Buxton imposed his authority.

"I feigned injury a couple of times in training to get back to have a game of snooker at the ground.

"'I'd say, 'Ooh, my hamstring's feeling a bit dodgy, I'd better pack up,' and be on the snooker table which got me a couple of tellings-off."

Despite being unable to resist the charms of the snooker room, not only did Starling prove himself to be a rich source of entertainment but he was also a very reliable last line of defence.

"It seems strange now that clubs have so many specialist goalkeeping coaches because for me everything was a natural instinct.

"I used to stay behind quite often for extra training and Mick, who was the goalie coach, would be constantly firing balls at me with John Haselden which was spot-on for me."

He may have been in the bad books when he was sent off after the final whistle by referee Colin Seel as Town tumbled out of the FA Cup against Darlington at Leeds Road for "foul and abusive language" but Buxton certainly rated him highly.

"He couldn't kick a ruddy ball but in terms of shot-stopping and goalkeeping Starling was excellent," Buxton said.

"I can't speak highly enough of him for his contribution on and off the pitch. Alan did a damned good job for me. He worked extremely hard in training, particularly on his goalkeeping with me.

"I knew what sort of character he was but he was a good person to have in the dressing room because he made people laugh like Joey Jones did when he arrived at Town. Starling was good but unfortunately he got injured and I needed a goalkeeper so I had to look elsewhere."

That rib injury was the beginning of the end for Starling, who was born in Barking, and had begun his career at Luton but only ended up between the sticks by chance while at Challney School, Luton.

"I became a goalkeeper purely by accident. It was in a school match when our goalie got injured and the PE teacher asked me to go in between the sticks and all of a sudden the trajectory of my life changed.

"It was pure luck. We lost something like 7-0 but I was really happy with my performance. We were 3-0 down when I went in between the sticks but I pulled off all sorts of saves.

"I did so well that our PE teacher told me afterwards that I'd have to stay in goal and I count myself as very fortunate because I got paid for doing something I would do as a hobby on a Saturday and Sunday anyway."

Goalkeeping came naturally for Starling, who would go on to play 126 times for Town.

"You don't have to be mad to be a goalkeeper but it certainly helps and I'd do anything to prevent a goal.

"I liked coming for crosses and I was never scared. It was always a natural reaction to go in where it hurts. It was instinctive.

"If a centre-forward was careering towards goal with the ball, then you'd dive at his feet. I never had second thoughts."

He made his first-team debut for Luton in March 1970 but then went out on loan to Torquay a year later before moving to Northampton in June 1972.

Life for a goalkeeper in those days was very different - a lot more uncompromising and almost brutal – compared to what their current contemporaries experience.

"We had gloves which were like table-tennis bats with all the pimples.

"Then Gordon Banks came out with gloves that were green cotton and everybody seemed to wear those but that's about all the protection we got.

"There was a lot more physical contact in those days but I don't think the way goalies are protected now is doing the game any favours.

"There are too many players feigning injury and diving. You think it's fatal and yet they bounce back up seconds later and they're running about again. That is frustrating.

"I took plenty of batterings when I was a goalie. I'll never forget the first time I bumped into Steve Kindon when I was at Luton because, crikey, that one ached.

"He was a big fella. He challenged for everything, I came out to get the cross. We collided, I was not particularly hurt but he was tough, I expected that sort of thing."

His performances at Luton caught the attention of England's bigger clubs and suddenly a move to Manchester United beckoned.

"There was talk about Alex Stepney leaving Old Trafford and Manchester United put in an offer of £18,500 bid for me for me and Alex Stock (Luton's manager) turned it down.

"Then that same week I did my knee in. I literally knelt down to pick the ball up and my cartilage snapped. I was only 17 and it was just my eighth game, so it all fell through which was a bit sad at the time.

"But crikey, Man U didn't half appeal to me. I was gutted. Stepney stayed put anyway so maybe everything happens for a reason."

He helped Northampton bounce back from having to re-apply for Football League status in 1972 and 1973 and win promotion from the old Fourth Division in 1976.

Starling also carved out a niche in Cobblers folklore by scoring from the penalty spot against Hartlepool as his club closed in on a top-four spot.

It was during that time that he used to travel up the M1 to Leicester City to train with England No1 Peter Shilton once a week to sharpen up his own skills.

"He worked so hard. He was tremendously fit. We'd take turns in goals with people knocking balls at us, discussing angles. It was tremendously beneficial, to me anyway."

There were other trappings of success as well in the shape of his first car or rather micro-car, the Italian-designed Iseta three-wheeler bubble car.

"We weren't allowed motorbikes but we were allowed to drive one of those when under 18 years of age. It was quite a sight. It even had a sunroof. I wish I still had it. It would be worth something now."

He was on the move again in March 1977 when manager Tom Johnston had Huddersfield pay £8,000 for his services as a replacement for the crocked Terry Poole and Dick Taylor.

Ten per cent of the transfer fee went to the Football Association and Starling pocketed five per cent but he didn't negotiate any signing-on fee and so there was just a little slice of the transfer fee left for him and £90-a-week wages.

"I remember getting to the ground and they told me to wait just inside the main entrance. Tom was tiny and ruddy scruffy and I thought the groundsman had come to get me rather than him.

"But I liked Tom. He was quite a character. I remember going into his office, thinking I would get a raise and it ended up being decreased by a fiver a week.

"That illustrates how he was. He didn't even try to justify it at all but bonuses did go up so you were expected to earn a little bit more.

"The club was always trying to find ways to avoid spending money and when I first arrived even my furniture was stored behind the goal underneath the scoreboard at the open end.

"It was a place that had its quirks but Leeds Road was a fabulous ground in comparison to the ones I was used to and I quickly fell in love with Huddersfield Town.

"It was a club with a fabulous history but when I arrived it was on its way down. But Town had tradition and you expected the club to climb back up just like Manchester United had done when they were relegated."

What he didn't expect were some of the off-the-field antics at Huddersfield.

"We were training at Canker Lane and we were a foot-deep in mud. Bobby Campbell was leading the way in the follow-the-leader run where you had to copy whatever he did.

"Anyway, he went into the place where Tom's car was parked, opened both back doors and every single one of us went through Tom's car, covered in mud.

"It seemed funny at the time among the lads. I thought this is great; I love this place. That first day of training was some introduction. Tom was there puffing away on his pipe. He couldn't believe what he was seeing."

Campbell, who died last year at the age of 60, had two spells at Town and as well as being a swashbuckling centre forward he was also usually at the centre of mischief.

"Bobby was buying a car and went into Lloyd's Bank in the town centre with the commercial manager who was into athletics and had a starting pistol.

"Bobby went into the bank with this pistol in his pocket, drew out a few hundred pounds, stuffed it into his pockets with notes hanging out and walked out with the pistol on show.

"It got reported and the police chased them. They were only messing about but someone had seen it and thought they were bank robbers. They let him off. You'd get shot these days."

According to Starling "many things make me chuckle to this day but are unsuitable for print" however "one incident can illustrate how stupid we were".

"We used to have big skips that we'd use for travelling away which you would put the kit and boots into.

"There was me and Bobby and a couple of others and we got one of the apprentices and locked him in this skip.

"And then we wheeled it out on to Leeds Road and left it in the middle of the busiest road in Huddersfield.

"How stupid is that? We were watching it and protecting it but, still, that was daft and dangerous."

Those lingering memories explain why Starling was so upset when Campbell, who became a Bradford City legend after leaving Town, took his own life.

"You would never expect that of Bobby. I used to bump into him quite often and it was only a couple of weeks before he did that when I saw him and he seemed to be in a good mood.

"He'd had some bad news from his GP. He thought he had cancer. And I think that all really got him down and it was his wife Paula (who introduced Starling to his own wife, Gillian) who found him in the garage. It was terrible, truly terrible."

Starling had to be mentally robust to handle life between the posts.

"Everyone remembers Leeds goalie Gary Sprake for throwing the ball into his own net at Anfield Liverpool fans in The Kop serenading him with the song 'Careless Hands'.

"That was very famous but I have to confess that I did something very similar at Swindon. I went to hurl the ball out to a teammate but it slipped out of my hand and went in off a post. The Swindon supporters were loving it.

"That was an extreme example but generally if a goalie makes a mistakes it's almost inevitably a goal whereas outfield players can make an error and there's anywhere up to ten people who can come to their rescue.

"It's almost masochistic but you remember the mistakes more than the saves and you never get over them. That wasn't because of any personal humiliation but because I'd let my own teammates down and that was absolutely galling.

"Whether you dropped a cross or the ball went through your legs it was awful because you'd let down your team and the supporters. But you had to try to forget it, and get on with the game.

"You had to clear your mind but then after the final whistle it was the time to re-live it over and over again. I'd wake up in the middle of the night thinking about it. That's an occupational hazard."

Starling was Town's reigning player of the year and first-choice goalie when the club embarked on the 1979/80 season.

"Mick was the sort of guy that you'd run through a brick wall for. He was a great man-manager and really good on the motivational front. You'd always do your very best for him.

"I liked Mick a lot and he was very strict which was fine with me. That was despite the fact that I fell foul of his disciplinary side quite a few times and got into trouble. I doubt I would have lasted nowadays because I used to enjoy myself too much.

"Our social life was fantastic. Johnny's nightclub was always the place to go with Slim on the door. We had VIP status which meant we didn't have to join the long queues on a Saturday night but we could walk to the front and be let straight in – one of the perks of the job.

"Things are completely different now to how they were then. All the lads had their funny points. It was brilliant and there was amazing camaraderie although it was a bit of a madhouse before Mick took over."

Starling, though, played a key role in Town's quest for silverware under Buxton and he played in the opening 22 fixtures of the 1979/80 campaign before injury meant he had to watch from the sidelines.

"It felt like I was part of something special. It was a fantastic feeling to wake up in the morning and look forward to what you're going to do.

"You couldn't have done anything better for a living and you'd be laughing so much as well but we were deadly serious when it mattered.

"Me and the defenders had complete understanding because we were all such good communicators and they were a pleasure to play with."

That was brought to a sudden halt after a 3-1 defeat at Torquay in December 1979, which proved to be his last game for the club.

"I got injured in training, going for a cross when I did my back in which is when they brought in Andy Rankin.

"I was very disappointed not to regain my place but pleased for Andy. These things happen. But he was a bloody good goalkeeper who did a great job."

Starling was released at the end of the season and in October 1980 was forced to announce his retirement from football due to injury.

He came out of retirement for a brief spell at Bradley Rangers in July 1983 and was then brought in as emergency cover by then Bradford City boss Trevor Cherry in December that year.

Nowadays, Starling who lives in The Mount, Huddersfield, is busy as national account manager for the Huddersfield-based Miles Group.

"Maybe if I'd been born 40 years later I could have made a lot more money but apart from that I don't feel as though I missed out on anything.

"I feel so lucky. I had a great rapport with the supporters. I'd love to re-live it all again. Huddersfield's been very kind to me but I'm still a comer-inner even though I've been here donkey's years."

....

Alan Starling reckons that he is lucky to be alive.

The father-of-two was called to Huddersfield Royal Infirmary for a routine screening just after turning 65 in April 2016

The test for abdominal aortic aneurysms (AAA) was to check the main arteries in the stomach area for potentially lethal aneurysms.

"I was invited in for a 'Triple A' examination and that turned out to be the biggest stroke of luck of my life.

"The scan found an aneurysm which was about to explode and could have led me to bleed to death within two minutes.

"It was so bad, they wouldn't let me go home and operated straight away. I was nine hours in surgery and a week in intensive care.

"I count myself as so very fortunate because the specialist was in that day and he was only in once a week. It was about to rupture."

The surgery was carried out by vascular surgeon consultant Anver Mahomed and Neeraj Bhasin and Starling was so grateful to them that he raised money for charity and still keeps in touch with his saviours.

And he continues to pay them back by encouraging people across Kirklees and Calderdale to live healthily.

"They were a dream team. The anesthetist was a Town supporter who came to see me every day.

"Now I talk to people with aneurisms that are manageable, talking to then about what can happen and why they need to change their diet and be sensible.

"They're nearly all smokers, which tells its own story. I used to smoke a packet of 20 a day but I've seen the light.

"I started when I was about 22. That was in the day when lots of players used to smoke and unfortunately I just got into it but it's a horrid, addictive habit.

"It's not long since I packed up. That major operation made my mind up. If I'm having a pint I still have the occasional herbal cigarette, which smells foul."

The accidental hero

Malcolm Brown

It was like something straight out of the movie Forrest Gump.

The Town fans who were stood in the Leeds Road terrace roared their approval when Malcolm Brown first charged down the wing because they had never seen anything like it

While they might not have shouted the immortal words 'Run, Forrest! Run' they did yell something pretty similar with 'Go on Mally' as they urged Brown to keep running and the speed merchant never looked back.

It would be a turning point not only in terms of right-back Brown's career but also Town's fortunes as he managed to combine the roles of solid defender and marauding winger to stunning effect.

His bold, bullocking runs become synonymous with Town's attacking flair under Mick Buxton but it is only now that Brown has revealed the reasons behind the discovery of his attacking mojo.

"I became an attacking full-back almost by accident and I have to admit it was all down to the crowd on the giant terrace," Brown said from his home in Droylesden, Greater Manchester.

"One day, I just started running with the ball, the crowd started cheering and got really got behind me and it began from there.

"It suddenly happened when I picked up the ball in defence and because I was quick, I burst forward and things just opened up in front of me.

"It certainly sounds like Forrest Gump. The fans started cheering me along and I just went further and further and further. It's a good job they encouraged me when I set off on a run because there was no stopping me after that.

"The fans would go on to kind of expect me to attack whenever I got on the ball which was lovely to hear and gave me the confidence to push forward. There weren't that many people watching us at first in those days but they didn't half show their appreciation.

"I loved playing on the far side, with our backs against the open end, running past the terrace. It was a great privilege to think that you're entertaining people. People were paying hard-earned money and they wanted you to give them something to shout about.

"It just showed what fan power could do. I loved having that rapport with the supporters which was completely new to me. Then the gaffer (Buxton) encouraged it and before I knew it I became one of our main attacking threats."

Brown joined Town when the club was at its lowest ebb but will go down as one of the club's greatest ever servants thanks to his swashbuckling wing play and long-striding, overlapping runs.

Turning defence into attack became an art form for Brown in his Town days as he racked up 259 consecutive matches between September 1978 when Town beat Doncaster 3-0 and May 1983 when Bradford won 3-1 at Valley Parade.

A string of personal accolades are testimony to the fact that he won acclaim from Town fans and fellow players alike thanks to his rampaging runs from deep defensive positions.

He received plenty of plaudits but there probably isn't a better summing-up of his game than that by Tom Marshall-Bailey in the *Huddersfield Examiner*.

'At 6ft 2in, Brown subverted all the stereotypes of modern-day offensive defenders, combining his attacking duties with a steely defensive resolve, making him effective in both halves of the pitch.

'Brown was a commanding presence who simply refused to be knocked off the ball. While most would consider the archetypal full-back to be smaller in stature, Brown's speed allied with an indefatigable stamina stood him out from the crowd.'

The towering Brown did not look like your average full-back but Buxton saw enough in a player inherited from predecessor Tom Johnston to effectively build a team around him.

Brown had been brought to Huddersfield from Bury, where his career started as an apprentice and then stalled, and Buxton's plan of action explains why he went back to Gigg Lane to sign Brian

Stanton two years later.

"I knew Brian from Bury and we really hit things off at Town once we got going.

"I know they were a lot better than us but it became almost like a Gary Neville and David Beckham type of partnership on the wing.

"If I went forward then Brian would fill in and do my defensive duties till I got back. We worked really well together.

"But things that happened on the pitch didn't happen by accident. We did a lot of team play in practice.

"If Brian received the ball wide, he'd look to play the ball into Ian Robins who might hold it up, he'd follow his pass and it worked a treat.

"It left a big hole for me to run into out wide on the wing for Robbo or Brian. Opposing teams found it difficult to defend against."

Brown began to learn his trade as an apprentice at Bury but only after he snubbed Manchester City's advances.

"I was playing for a kids' team (a nursery side for Preston North End) and funnily enough in the last game of the season there was a Bury scout there and one from City.

"The City scout told me to come down the following Wednesday just to see them and I had no idea what for but the Bury asked me to go earlier and when I went along he said they wanted me to become an apprentice.

"I took my chance while it was there and apparently the City guy wasn't very happy about it because he just wanted me down at their place the following week but I didn't have a clue what they were thinking."

It was at Bury where his potential as a full-back was inadvertently spotted.

"I've got a lot to be grateful for with Bury. I started off as a midfielder, well I thought I was a midfielder, but then fate lent a hand in my life, which it has done every now and again.

"We were playing a game at Gigg Lane, a friendly against Scunthorpe reserves, and they had nobody to play left-back so they asked me to step in. I said, 'Bloody hell, I can't play left-back, I'm right-footed.'

"Anyway my protests fell on deaf ears and I thought I did pretty well but others people thought I did really well and that's how I became a full-back. Then they switched me to right-back and so it happened purely by accident.

"I'd found my true calling. It was that little bit of luck that lots of footballers need because there are so many pitfalls waiting for kids coming through the game when there is so much competition for places. It helps when you get little breaks but you've got to make the most of them."

Brown also had to graft as an apprentice with the hard labour that was then seen to turn boys into men from the age of 16 to 18.

"We went in early morning and even before a ball was kicked we had loads of chores to get through.

"There was making sure all the kit was out for the players and then carting all the equipment needed for training which took place about 500 yards away from the stadium.

"We'd have to lug all the cones, markers and barrels on the back of a cart and then push it down to the training ground and then cart everything back afterwards.

"Then there was the sweeping of the stands because the club didn't employ cleaners and then there was the final thing, which was cleaning the senior players' boots.

"It was a really good grounding. It kept your feet on ground. It stopped you getting too ahead of yourself."

There was no chance of that happening to Brown who suddenly found himself facing the proverbial football scrapheap when Bury released him as an 18-year-old.

"It was the manager, Bob Smith, who felt I needed to grow up a bit and he was right.

"I was a quiet, shy kid. I guess I was a bit of a mummy's boy who needed to get out in to the big wide world and that did me good. Bob did me a favour but I didn't know it at the time."

The road to Huddersfield would become his Brown's only option.

"When Bob told me it was time to move on he cushioned the blow by saying two clubs were interested in me.

"There was Huddersfield and there was Torquay but they dropped out at the last minute because they didn't have any money left.

"Their manager rang me up and said they'd signed a player and had used up all their budget on him so he was really sorry but he couldn't afford my wages.

"So fate had taken a hand again and I went to Huddersfield which was the only choice I had to stay in the game.

"Tom Johnston signed me and he was tight with his money but he was all right by me because he found me a few quid to buy a car because he knew I had to travel over from Manchester."

Brown made his Town debut in front of 4,435 fans in a goalless draw against Swansea at the start of the 1977/78 season. He was one of the players who thrived when Buxton took over from Johnston and heralded a sea-change.

"People would knock him but he was a nice old man who had a good pedigree.

"He'd won a couple of promotions with York, so he must have known what he was doing and how to deal with players and sort out teams.

"There were plenty of decent players on the books but we weren't the best of organised sides. That all changed when the gaffer took over. It was like chalk and cheese.

"I'll always remember his first training session because of his attitude. It was a case of 'this is my first training session so you'd better make it good'.

"So straight away you get the message that this guy's not going to stand any messing.

"But he wasn't just about discipline. We were doing shooting practice and I cracked one in from 25 yards. He loved it and that got me into his good books."

Brown took responsibility for free-kicks down the right flank and was forced to hone them as "we lost the will to live" in long, drawn-out practice sessions.

"The gaffer would have us perfecting free-kicks, especially were we touched the ball and knocked it in near-post, for hours on end.

"We'd be out until two o'clock on a Friday afternoon, which was an awful long time in the mind of a footballer.

'We were like, 'flipping heck, haven't we got a game tomorrow, we'll be shattered.' He demanded that everything to be as spot-on perfect as you could possibly hope to be.

"And just when we thought we'd sorted things out, he'd have us do it just once more to check it wasn't a fluke."

There was also a fear-factor around the dressing room that came into play under Buxton.

"Footballers have to have a certain amount of fear and the gaffer ensured that was the case.

"Working with Tom and then the gaffer showed me that it's important that if players don't pull their fingers out and do things right then there will be consequences

"(Sir Alex) Ferguson, (Brian) Clough and (Bill) Shankly showed that fear is one of the greatest things a manager can have up his sleeve."

Ferguson had the hairdryer treatment when he blasted players while Buxton relied on his right foot.

"He could lose his rag. There were times when he'd throw a cup of tea around the dressing room but one half-time still stands out.

"We used to have a table in the dressing room for a rub before the game and next to it there was a box with all the medical stuff in it, packed into little drawers.

"He came in and wasn't best pleased . He put his foot against the table, booted it and all the drawers shot out and everything was strewn all over the place.

"We all did our best to keep a straight face even though we were killing ourselves inside but no one dared laugh."

Medical matters also sprang to mind for Brown when the team flew to Guernsey on a mid-season break that Buxton used to punctuate the football calendar.

The flight from the Midlands was delayed and the final leg of the journey from Jersey was completed in three groups on a small shuttle service.

"I was nervous when we got to the airport because I'd never flown before.

"I remember walking across the Tarmac and there were all these nice, new jets and I was wondering which one are we getting on.

"But then I saw a plane that looked like something from the Dambusters film, with its four propellers, which looked like it was falling apart, and that was ours. All the seats were ripped. I was frightened to death.

"Alan Starling sat a few seats behind me, winding me up because he'd got wind of the fact that I'd never flown before. When we headed down the runway, he said 'Mally don't worry – there's no way this plane is going to get off the ground.'

"Everyone had a laugh at my expense, saying I looked like a ghost and passing me sick bags, but I didn't mind in the end because I was just grateful to be in one piece. Anyway, there was a wonderful spirit amongst us and that sort of ribbing was important."

There was something about planes, training and automobiles for Brown and his Town teammates.

"A load of us came in together from the Manchester area but there was a problem with our driver for the day so we kindly got a lift back from Dave Sutton.

"We were getting in when Sutty said, 'I must tell you I've got a bit of a leak in my exhaust, a bit of a hole.'

"We all thought fair enough but there was quite a weight in the car, with me and Keith Hanvey and Peter Fletcher and Ian Robins and the car was struggling.

"We started to go up the hill and the Sutty was going down the gears when smoke started coming into the foot wells. Then it was billowing out. We had to wind the windows down so Sutty could see where he was going and so we could breathe.

"It's those sorts of incidents and going for a pint together after home games at the Junction pub that bonded us. It's not rocket science.

If you get a good set of lads who can play a bit and you're prepared to work hard and are well organised you don't need a lot more."

Off-the-field things were on the up for Brown as he got married and moved into a place he could call his own when the newly-weds bought a bungalow for £24,000.

Brown scored twice and created countless goals as Town soared to promotion but it is a home game against Scunthorpe rather than the 2-1 win over Hartlepool that clinched silverware which stands out.

"I remember the Hartlepool game being a struggle but the one I remember more clearly is the 1-0 win over Scunthorpe that got us promoted.

"I had a free-kick. I knocked the ball in and Ian Robins met it with a brilliant header, so all that hard work on the training ground had paid off.

"But what I remember most is how quiet the ground was. It was as if the supporters were on edge. They'd seen the bad times and they were worried as if it too good to be true. It was so quiet it was eerie."

Brown pipped 25-goal leading scorer Robins and the talismanic Steve Kindon to the Hargreaves Memorial Trophy as the club's player of the year award. He was also voted into the divisional Professional Footballers' Association team of the year along with Robins.

He was just getting started because from 1979-1983, Brown was voted into four successive PFA teams of the year, the latter alongside rising stars in the shape of Chelsea striker Kerry Dixon and Norwich's Steve Bruce.

He won a place in the 1990/1991 PFA team while at Stockport, spending a season at Rochdale before retiring in 1992 and training to become a driving instructor which is how he still makes a living.

"I'm dead busy with the driving school but I'll be making sure that I see Town as much as possible in the Premier League.

"I was a Man United fan as a kid and I'd have always loved to have played for them but Town are my team because of the great times I had there.

"We had a re-union at the club a while back and I was really surprised and touched by how many fans turned up to join us.

"Town will always mean a lot to me. Not just because of the success we had but because of the laughs we had in the canteen and because it was a happy family club, right from Nellie Thompson to the board of directors.

"It was also the place where I grew up and became a man and a professional footballer.

"The best thing that ever happened to me was crossing paths with Mick Buxton and that was down to fate. Mick was like a father to me. He made me a player and with John Haselden, he blended us into a team that never feared anyone."

....

Malcolm Brown's sterling performances in a Town shirt were enough to attract the attention of Newcastle United and at the age of 28 and in the prime of his career, he moved to St James' Park in a £100,000-deal in 1983.

"If you're in the game and you don't want to see how far you can go then there's no point being a pro footballer. I didn't know if I'd be good enough to play at the top level but I wanted to find out."

There had even been talk linking Brown with a £250,000-move to Sunderland and Liverpool were also rumoured to be interested but his hopes of establishing himself as a First Division player were short-lived as he suffered a devastating injury at Newcastle when he snapped an Achilles tendon.

"It was a total accident. It was the second of third day of pre-season training, we were doing some springs – knees, chest and then you sprinted ten or 20 yards - but as I landed I just felt something snap at the back of my ankle.

"When I saw the surgeon I described it as though someone had cracked a whip on the back of my ankle and apparently that's the *telltale sign.*

"It was a horrendous injury. It took me two or three years to recover and robbed me of the chance to find out how far I could go."

"I remember when I left Town, Phil Neal was packing it in at and Keith Hanvey said I'd play for England so it was a massive disappointment. Still, though, I feel like I've been very lucky."

He was forced to miss the whole of the 1983-84 season but despite his injury setback, Brown recovered enough to have a strong season on Tyneside, playing in 39 games out of 42, before returning to Leeds Road.

"Jack Charlton came in and said you're going to play in every pre-season game and I thought he was joking because I was still limping around the place. But I did and then played almost all the whole season, which I regard as a massive achievement.

"Before I played I had to stand in a hot bath because my ankle was so stiff that was the only way to get it moving and then after the game I'd go into the bar and I'd be limping like an old man."

A dog's life

Dave Sutton

It was the piercing sound of wolf whistling from across the road as they were getting into bed that really did it for Dave and Jacqueline Sutton.

The young couple found themselves living in a dingy club flat above the Town shop on Leeds Road when he joined the Terriers on loan in March 1978.

"We weren't sure what we were letting ourselves in for when we came to Huddersfield," said Dave.

"But I was really wondering if we'd made a really bad move when we were taken to the flat they'd set aside for us above the old club shop.

"Nellie Thompson (the club cleaner), bless her, had spent a few days trying to clear the place up for us and make it nice but it was still a right old mess.

"There were curtains hanging off the rails. It was an eyesore and it just didn't feel homely at all.

"It was on a right noisy main road and things were so bad that we got wolf whistles from across the road when we were getting into bed."

They had tried to laugh off the depressing living quarters but it was whistling that was the final straw for the recently-weds and Town manager Tom Johnston was given an ultimatum.

"You'd never get a senior player staying in a place like so I went in and spoke to Tom and told him, 'If you don't find us somewhere else sharpish, we're off.'

"He got the club to put us in a bed-and-breakfast near the town centre which was much more suitable but it wasn't the best of starts.

"I found out that they'd always try to get away with the cheapest option because at the time the club was struggling for money.

"You get used to that sort of thing. It's part of life, character-building and it's the sort of experience you can look back on and have a laugh about.

"It was far from funny at the time but I wasn't going to throw the toys out of the pram because it was a chance to play for Huddersfield."

Then on Plymouth's books, he was persuaded to up sticks and leave Devon for Yorkshire by Johnston who set up a meeting with Sutton when Town were on the south coast to play Torquay, clearly impressed by what he saw when Sutton faced Town while he was on a two-month loan with Reading.

"I was only on £23 a week and the missus and me were living in a flat and we didn't even have a car so they paid our train fare up.

"We stuck all our possessions in a suitcase, apart from a £60-fridge we put in storage, and ended up at Huddersfield train station.

"I'd wanted to get back up North but this was like coming into a different world when you've been down south.

"I'd been up to Huddersfield before when I was in the Plymouth squad and what you notice is that stone work was black.

"Even compared to Lancashire, it had a different feel about it but we got used to it."

It was people like Nellie who made him feel right at home and after just one month on loan at Town he signed a permanent deal and his wages were trebled.

The £15,000 transfer fee represented the first three weeks' proceeds of Town's new 'Lucky Horoscope Lottery'.

"The people at the ground were really friendly and that welcome helped. They were brilliant, especially Nellie who was a star.

"We used to get these big tins of Nescafe coffee, and I'm not sure if I was one of her favourites but if the tin was half-full, she always used to slip it to me to take home.

"If were late for training, we'd nip in through a side-entrance and then dart into the kit room and Nellie would cover for us so we didn't get into trouble.

"Jimmy Robson (the reserves manager) was always on the main door waiting for us, so we'd sneak in then walk out with kit on as if we'd been there ages. It was only to avoid a 50-pence fine but it seemed like a lot of money."

Sutton said he "thought the world of people behind the scenes".

"There was Ray (Chappell) the groundsman who used to moan like buggery if anyone touched his pitch and if you dared to criticise it he'd not speak to you for ages. So we used to say it looked like a meadow just to wind him up.

"And there was big Fred (Elms) the club joiner and repair man who'd actually made the wooden goals, and a little fella, his helper, who did all the work around the ground who had a ridiculous amount of fingers half cut-off. They were real characters.

"Our dressing room was a bit like an open house but when we had to focus on work on match days it was deadly serious."

Initially, Sutton hooked up with Arnie Sidebottom in the heart of Town's defence, a partnership that was short-lived as the former Manchester United player, who played cricket for Yorkshire and England, broke his arm in one of their first games together.

Sutton, who is now director of football at North West Counties Football League side Burscough and runs the family business, Sooty's Plants, came in when the Johnston era was drifting towards an end.

"He was a gentleman but the more experienced players took advantage of him; they took the Mickey. They got away with murder at times.

"There was one incident that stood out. They opened Tom's car and everyone went through the back seat and everyone followed him.

"Things like that, which on the surface sound like harmless fun, just shouldn't happen to managers.

"You can't imagine players wearing dirty kit doing that to someone like Bill Shankly. There was no discipline and little work ethic but that seeps in at a lot of clubs and it's why managers get fired."

Sutton had already won over Mick Buxton before he was promoted from coach to manager.

"He always rated my attitude and actually said to the rest of the players that if they'd had my attitude then we'd do a lot better which was a bit embarrassing.

"He said that in front of everyone when I was on loan so it didn't go down too well with the players but I just did things right. You train as you play. I've never been the most gifted player but I had a big heart to do a decent job.

"There was also the snooker table so I thought this isn't a bad club when I first got there. The first thing that Mick did was to get rid of it because there were too many injured players having games of snooker. And he had a point. They were more interested in playing snooker than knuckling down."

According to Sutton, "everything changed" when Buxton took the helm and "life got a lot harder" but the players' fitness improved amid a better-organised set-up.

"It was very up-to-date. There were circuits and weights. We trained two afternoons a week a lot and pre-season was murder.

"There were hundreds of shuttles, long runs and a lot of hill work. Those hills were so tough that I'd been using the grass to pull myself up. That's how bad it was.

"It used to be a great feeling getting back after training and having a bath and cup of tea. It felt like heaven. But you could hardly walk trying to get in the car.

"Our fitness levels shot up. They were a lot better than other teams'. We seemed to do well late on in games and even when we weren't playing well we'd hang in there."

It was probably because training was so demanding that Buxton allowed Sutton to bring pet Labrador, Babe, along to training sessions to ease the pain.

"I used to take Babe to training with me whenever I could and sometimes took her into the dressing room. Mick wasn't bothered.

"All the lads would make a right fuss of her. I'd tie her up by one of the goalposts when we started and it wouldn't stop moaning. John

Haselden would go mad.

"It was the sort of thing that Mick allowed because he knew it brought people together. Underneath it all, he had a soft heart and a soft spot for the dog."

Babe certainly gave Sutton's teammates a chance to laugh at his expense.

"Most days we had to run down to Leeds Road playing fields for training but on Fridays we'd drive down.

"So I took Babe and three of the lads and then I put her back in until we'd done the warm-up. Once the lads decided to run back because she'd done a big shit on the back seat.

"There was also the time Babe attacked my car and almost got me into trouble with the police. She ripped the foam dashboard to shreds and pulled off the electrics.

"I was getting it scrapped at the Cooper Bridge scrapyard when I got pulled over by the police. I told them I knew the car was not roadworthy but that was because of Babe the vandal. They were very understanding."

Your average football club car park will nowadays be full of costly cars but even though Sutton and his colleagues were unable to splash out, living outside the fast lane left him with an endless supply of anecdotes.

"Every car I had in those days was second-hand and I got a Skoda off my sister which was a right state.

"We were living in Heckmondwike and the weather was that bad I had to stick my head out the window to see where I was going because the heating didn't work.

"And once it was so cold all my hair was iced up by the time I arrived at the ground. The missus and me used to have hot-water bottles that we'd take into the car.

"Then there was a pale-blue Ford Escort 1100. Before training I had to take out the spark plugs and warm them up over the gas hob so they would fire properly. It was crazy.

"Someone's car broke down and I had to take all the Manchester lads back to their cars. I nearly gassed them out because all the fumes were coming up through a hole in the floor of the car."

There was also an Austin Maxi that he bought off a neighbour.

"When we went to the Town Hall for the civic reception to celebrate winning the Fourth Division title, I had to fill it up with petrol and bomb like fuck down Leeds Road before it ran out because the tank had a great big hole in it.

"I needed a spare can of petrol as well. I still remember as we got on the coach, looking at this stream of petrol running across the car park and it started underneath my car. It just shows how much things have changed."

Sutton was brought up in the Lancashire village of Tarleton, between Preston and Southport, and was studying for his O-levels and playing local football when he was invited to take part in trials at Liverpool.

He did well enough to sign schoolboy forms with the Anfield club along with future Liverpool players David Fairclough and Colin Irwin.

Sutton played for Liverpool's A and B teams and could have signed amateur forms but started taking A-levels with a career as a chartered engineer in mind before he signed for Plymouth, then of the Third Division.

"They were playing up at Carlisle, they picked me up on M61 with my big suitcase and at the age of 16 I went all the way down to Plymouth."

The football came thick and fast as he worked his way into the first team at Home Park.

"On the Thursday, we had to travel by train back and forth from London because we were playing in the football combination against Crystal Palace, who had Dave Swindlehurst up front for them.

"I was told to make sure I had a rest but I still had to go in on the Friday, do all my jobs at nine o'clock and then I heard I was in the first team against Oldham (who included Ian Robins and legendary striker Andy Lochhead) that night and this was all after travelling back from London.

"I slept in his office before I played but we drew 0-0 and I had a great game (alongside veterans Bobby Saxton and Jim Furnell) and on the Sunday I had to play in the Plymouth and District Youth Cup Final and then on the Monday we played York City.

"People complain about having too many matches to play and, yes, it was manic but it just shows how, if you want something badly enough, you can achieve it."

Sutton played 61 times for the Pilgrims and had a loan spell at Reading who were on their way to better things with the likes of Lawrie Sanchez, Neil Webb, Kerry Dixon and Gary Peters on their books.

He resisted the offer to join Reading on a permanent basis and headed to Yorkshire and there was no stopping Sutton and his teammates once they got up a head of steam in that 1979-80 season.

"We were all on roughly £100 a week and we didn't have two penn'orth to rub together but there was great comradeship.

"We all had a few pints together and had a great laugh. We even laughed at how tight the club was. We classed ourselves as the mortgage players because we were paying the mortgage.

"We'd get £10 in appearance money and win or draw bonuses but they were crafty so-and-sos because new lads got £10 per week rather than appearance.

"So we'd get £20 for two wins and new lads got half that because they didn't read their contracts properly. Little things like that showed how desperate they were to save money.

"We used to get £20 to put to a pair of boots. That was it. Money was so tight I used to shit myself knocking on Mick Buxton's door asking for £20 towards new boots.

"He'd look at you as if you'd committed a crime. My boot of choice was the Puma King which were £50 a go. They were made out of kangaroo skin. I loved them. I've still got a pair now.

"Mick liked to keep things tight. He could have treated us a bit better and been more generous but he probably thinks that with the quality of player we were that he was too generous."

Sutton may not have always seen eye-to-eye with Buxton but still appreciated his managerial acumen.

"Mick liked the old Burnley way of playing football, which was similar to the way I'd been brought up at Plymouth. We were a good attacking side and you always tended to know what everyone was going to do.

"Tony Waiters, who was my manager at Plymouth, was way ahead of his time, coaching-wise, he was staff coach at Lilleshall, and we had Allan Brown who was Brian Clough's mentor – who was ex-army sergeant major.

"At the start of pre-season, he made us do a 25-mile run from Looe to Polperro along the cliff path.

"He did all this shadow-play, which Terry Venables took on board, and Mick Buxton did the same, probably because him and Alan had both been at Burnley.

"With shadow-play the ten outfield players attack your goalkeeper. He kicks the ball out and all the players do certain runs.

"So if you're the centre-half you know what you've got one or two options and others know what space to run into. When it came to overlapping, the winger moves inside to create space. If you have a free-kick in a certain spot you know exactly what free-kick you're going to do."

Under such a well-drilled regime, there was nowhere to hide if things went wrong.

"We all knew our roles when we played. You couldn't get away with anything. If you made a mistake there was none of this trying to blame other people.

"If a full-back let anyone cross a ball they knew they'd be in trouble with me back in the dressing room and if I let anyone have a free header or I dived in on a striker I'd say sorry.

"Some might need a kick up the arse but I didn't. I had a stinker against Watford in the Milk Cup when John Barnes was playing, and he was brilliant. Mick knew he didn't need to say anything.

"I was over-critical of my own game. You want the team to win but if it's no good for me when the team win and I didn't play well. That's how bad it was for me personally.

"Even now if I don't play well at five-a-side I hate it. I still want to be the best player on the pitch. That's just the way I've always been, even in the training."

Sutton, an ever present in the 1979/80 season until the final match of the campaign, when he was concussed, struck up an important central defensive partnership with Keith Hanvey.

They also got in amongst the goals as the hard work practicing set-pieces paid off in style.

"It was the next-to-last game against Torquay and I tell everyone who asks that I scored the 98th and 99th goal and should have had the 100th against my name.

"Another corner came in and I connected again and the ball was going right for the top corner but someone just managed to flick it away. I could have got a hat-trick and how the hell I didn't go in, to this day I don't know.

"I was all set to put things right against Hartlepool but I ended up going off with concussion at half-time. I felt like I'd been hit by a brick.

"It was a blur then and it is now. It was a clash of heads and so I can't remember too much but it was a great achievement. It was a bit nerve-wracking and so it was a big relief in the end."

Things turned slightly sour due to money afterwards and Sutton went on the transfer list shortly after promotion.

"As we went to the Town Hall on the coach, Keith Longbottom (the club chairman) was going up and down the aisle saying to the players 'now don't be asking for too much of a rise' and this was just after we'd got promoted.

"I wanted a £10 rise for going up but Mick wouldn't have it and said they'd put me on the transfer list instead. The thing was, he wouldn't give me an extra tenner but they wanted £100,000 for me. In the end I signed a new two-year deal for an extra fiver."

He helped Town to promotion again in 1981 but his career took a turn for the worse went he broke his leg at Manchester City's old Maine Road ground.

"I had a knee injury and I knew it wasn't right. But I thought, blow it. You know, 40,000 fans inside Maine Road, I won't feel the pain," he told the Lancashire Post.

"We were awarded a penalty in the first minute and Huddersfield were 1-0 up. Anyway, we broke clear again, and as I was chasing a ball I was tackled by Derek Parlane. I looked down and my foot was hanging off. It was an awful sight."

Sutton's tibia and fibula were fractured and he underwent surgery before the game had finished. "We were well looked after. We weren't living in the dark ages and John Haselden worked me really hard in my rehabilitation to get me playing again."

Despite being offered a new contract, Sutton would eventually leave Town in June 1985 for Bolton in a £12,000-deal which meant "I got three times as much" but in "hindsight I shouldn't have gone."

After three years at Bolton he moved to Rochdale on a free transfer before being forced to quit playing due to injury but he would eventually spend three years as manager at Spotland.

His transition into management was made easier thanks to coaching courses he followed while playing at Town.

"We did the Coca Cola coaching courses, two nights a week on Astroturf, because John Haselden always encouraged us to get stuck into them with an eye on the future.

"Someone came up to me at the lads' re-union at the Town ground and said, 'You won't believe it but you coached me down at Leeds Road when I was a young lad.' It was Dean Hoyle."

....

It is difficult to imagine a more searing insight into the ups and downs of management than the one Dave Sutton provided to his local paper

"The hardest part of managing was losing games. I'd take it so much to heart," the former Rochdale boss told the Lancashire Post in 2008.

"It was horrendous - like a black cloud descending over me on a Saturday night.

"I'd be distraught sometimes. It wasn't fair on my family. I have a wife and three lovely daughters and it was really hard on them.

"In management you are so reliant on other people, and most footballers are selfish, self-centred people.

"I remember the late Billy Bremner saying, 'Dave, the trouble with the modern-day player is that they all let you down eventually', and they do.

"Management is such an intense experience. It is hard to convey what it is really like. It is true about the drink. It is a prop for some managers, a pressure valve I suppose.

"When I think about what I drank at Rochdale, I come out in a hot sweat. I'd have a few whiskeys before the game, and that was normal. Then, win, lose or draw, I'd have a few more afterwards.

"Maybe it wasn't very professional, but that's the way it was then. I can definitely understand why drink does become a problem in management.

"Sometimes it was like an arrogance. You know, 'I'll have a few whiskeys, it isn't going to affect me'. It was like bravado when things were going well. Then you'd use it to drown your sorrows when things went badly.

"It was all going a bit stupid. I could be brutally outspoken and said some things I shouldn't have. I was diagnosed with Meniere's Disease. The doctors told me it was a condition brought on by stress and it affects your balance.

"I was at Stoke Reserves versus Burnley, and afterwards Jimmy Lumsden (ex-Preston coach), invited me in the boardroom. I took a sip of coffee and collapsed. Jimmy probably saved my life that night because 10 minutes later I'd have been on the M6 driving home. I had an operation a few days later and, thankfully, it cured me.

"There was a lot of stress. Sometimes I couldn't sleep at night because of the pressure. You'd go in a board meeting and it was like Mastermind. "You'd be sat in this giant, black chair with 20 guys firing questions at you. It could be a mad, mad world."

Sutton was Rochdale's manager from 1991 to 1994 before taking charge at Chorley where part-time players earned more than he did at Huddersfield.

One player who was worth every penny was future £1-million Bristol City striker Lee Trundle who was signed from Burscough in a £22,500 deal after Sutton spotted him while he was playing in a trial for Preston.

"People laughed their heads off when I said that Lee Trundle would be the first non-league £1m player. He was the best talent I've ever worked with and he should have played for England. I played against Kevin Keegan and Chris Waddle, but they didn't have the skill of Lee Trundle."

On a wing and a prayer

Keith Hanvey

It was on a golf course and it was in the middle of summer when Keith Hanvey began to fear that he had made one of the worst decisions of his life.

Hanvey had just joined Huddersfield from Grimsby in July 1978 to be closer to his family home in Manchester but he soon started regretting the move.

"It was a lot like a holiday camp when I went there under Tom Johnston. In the first week, we played golf, we went crown green bowling and then we did something else just as leisurely.

"I thought: 'Oh my God - what the hell have I done?' It was like a bit of a fun club. Football wasn't the paramount thing on their minds. It's all right having fun but let's win and have fun.

"There's a time and a place for golf but we were on the golf course when we should have been grafting at Leeds Road Playing Fields as this was pre-season and you've got to work hard to get yourself ready for the slog ahead.

"There was lots of chuntering behind the scenes and there was a band who were just there to have a laugh at the club's expense but it wasn't funny."

Things didn't get much better once Hanvey settled down.

"We had a snooker table there and lads would say they had a slight knock and come back from training early and they'd all be playing snooker when the rest of us returned.

"It was a friendly enough place but it was a poor excuse for a football club. There was something that was just fundamentally wrong - just the opposite of Grimsby, which had been fundamentally disciplined.

"The priority was supposed to be success but it didn't seem as though that was the club's main focus. It made me think 'no wonder they'd had such a poor spell over the last few years'. The attitude wasn't right. It was very lax.

"I actually bought the snooker table because Mick said that's going when he became manager and I said 'oh well and I might just buy it but I had nowhere to put it and so I had to put it in storage for18 months. I had to build an extension to get the thing in."

It was all a culture shock for Hanvey both off the field and on it as the 6ft 2in central defender found himself thrust into unchartered territory in Town's first team.

"They'd already signed Chris Topping from York so I ended playing on the left-hand side of midfield. I was more or less a winger."

"In friendlies, Tom played me out wide because he wanted me to get on the far post and knock in a few crosses.

"I thought 'no way, I've never played here before.' I must admit I thought 'what on earth, am I doing here?' quite a few times."

It was not long before he was put out of his misery when Mick Buxton took over from Johnston.

"I could sense Mick was exasperated with the general attitude around the place when he was Tom's coach.

"There was a total transformation when Mick took over but his first words to me were: 'What on earth are you doing out there on the left wing?'

"I had to tell him that I wasn't sure because I'd not played there in my life before I came to Huddersfield. I felt like the proverbial fish out of water on the left wing.

"I'm just glad Mick saw sense. He stuck me back at centre-half and that's how it stayed with me and Dave Sutton with Chris as back-up. It was a case of better late than never."

That helped Hanvey deal with the mixed emotions of seeing Grimsby win promotion in 1978.

"It was of those situations where you just click because your styles of play and strengths are complementary.

"I was the reader and I used to set up the back four and Dave was the very brave winner of the ball so I was the sweeper-come-organiser of the defence.

"I used to say 'Dave you're ugly so you might as well go and head the balls.' For six years Dave was my partner at the back so I don't think he can have taken offence."

Hanvey was born in Manchester and after missing out on taking his 11-plus due his family moving home, he showed enough academic promise to eventually earn a place at North Manchester Grammar School.

"I was very much into football and cricket as a youngster and I knuckled down at grammar school but as I progressed I was convinced I was going to make one of those sports my livelihood.

"I was on Manchester City's books from the age of 14 but my parents didn't want me to sign on as an apprentice.

"They wanted me to get my education first: 'Football? No way. Get your education first.' It's amazing how different it was from the current day and age."

He excelled as a cricketer, representing Manchester and Lancashire and receiving a special award from England legend Brian Statham for taking a hat-trick while playing for his city.

"I stayed on at grammar school to study A-levels which meant I missed the opportunity of progressing earlier with an apprenticeship at Man City.

"I lost my way at City because I had to play for the grammar school team at weekends. That was a strict order and that's why I left the school.

"As a compromise, I said I'd play one year for you and then the next year I was going to play for City's A and B teams at weekends because otherwise I'd ruin my prospects of a career in football."

Hanvey was on a collision course with the school and in those draconian days there was only going to be one winner.

"I ended up having a run-in with the headmaster which meant I had to leave North Manchester Grammar. That was because I didn't turn up for the first match of the season in my second year of A-levels.

"My form teacher, who was also my geology teacher, had thrown a school football shirt at me and said 'you're captain on Saturday, be there' and I was never going to be there because I was going to play for City.

"I came in on the Monday morning and he said 'I'm not teaching you.' That's what they could get away with in those days. It had been on my mind for quite a few days but we had a set-to. I had to leave and finished my A-levels at Ashton-Under-Lyne College."

It proved to be a wise move and he made up for lost time by playing for Bury rather than City.

"I had to get back up to speed with the rest of the players but it couldn't have gone any better and I made good progress.

"I'd just played in a practice match one Saturday morning when Joe Mercer and Malcolm Allison walked over to me and asked if I'd like to sign on for City on professional terms. Too right I did. I'll never forget that moment."

Hanvey made his senior debut for City in the old Texaco Cup against Scottish side Airdrie in September 1971 and he had been made substitute in a First Division game against Everton when he experienced one of those life-changing episodes.

"I didn't get on against Everton because Tommy Booth was fit so I had to play in the reserves up at Newcastle and broke my thigh within ten minutes and my career trajectory changed.

"It took me two-and-a-half years to get over what was an accidental collision with a lad called Stewart Barrowclough who was their flying winger. He was a spindly, boney lad and he just went into my thigh."

The long road to recovery began on the A1 as the team bus meandered past Scotch Corner.

"I couldn't get my trousers on so I just had to put my leg up on the back row of the bus, ligged out and put up with the bumpy ride home. I felt horrendous.

"I didn't go to hospital and limped home, didn't sleep a wink and went the next day. There was an X-ray and they found out I'd broken my thigh and the muscles had been torn apart by the impact.

"I'd broken my leg previously and you're back after 12 weeks but this was never right which was because of the muscle clinging to the bone that made it so much worse.

"I had a major operation six months later to sort out the calcifying of muscle on my bone when it didn't repair which is why it took so long.

"I joke that if it wasn't for the injury I'd have had 100 England caps on my wall at home – no question! But on a serious note that was the curtailment of any high-level prospects I had."

Hanvey went on loan to Swansea but when he came back to his hometown, Allison had been sacked as manager and his replacement, John Bond, "didn't fancy me."

"My dad (James) had cancer at time so I wanted to come back to Manchester and decided to leave City for Rochdale, which was probably rash, but I wanted to play football.

"I was sold to Grimsby to pay the VAT bill at Rochdale. I was told I was going by the manager. It was different at that time. The club was the be-all and end-all. Players had little say in their futures."

Hanvey might not have enjoyed the travelling but he knew he was on to a good thing on the east coast.

"There was no M18 in those days and so Grimsby was a two-and-a-half-hour drive from home on a good day and I ended up losing loads of money because I seemed to get fined every week for turning up late for training.

"I trained at City once or twice a week but when I travelled to Grimsby I always seemed to get stuck in a traffic bottleneck around a little place called Guness which I blame for most of my wages going on fines."

His spell with the Mariners may have been short-lived but provided Hanvey with a taste of things to come.

"Grimsby had been struggling at the bottom but there was a flurry of transfer activity after we'd been relegated and it turned into a club on the up.

"We had decent side, with a winning mentality, and I enjoyed the football side of things but I wanted to be closer to home for personal reasons.

"Grimsby wanted to keep me and they offered me a three-year deal. I knew I was leaving a good club but it was just family life. I wanted to see what was happening elsewhere and I was wanting to get back to the Manchester area."

Huddersfield came in for Hanvey when Johnston learned he was going to be a free agent.

"I nearly became famous because I was going to be the first freedom of contract court case between two clubs when I came to Huddersfield.

"Grimsby wouldn't have let me go normally but they were strange times with freedom of contract.

"That case was going to be in Manchester one Monday morning and I was due to be the first case but they agreed the fee as I was just setting off.

"Grimsby wanted 75 grand for me and Town had offered a bag of chips and an annual pass to Johnny's nightclub. In the end they came to their senses and they agreed a fee of about £15,000 and I was on my way to Huddersfield."

Hanvey had a few options but chose Huddersfield, where he was paid a basic £100 a week, because he saw potential that was only realised once Buxton got going.

"Mick made things very regimented and disciplined and we used to work on set-pieces hour after hour after hour which was really tedious.

"Everyone moaned because a footballer's life isn't a hectic one. You come in for ten o'clock and you hopefully get away for about 1-1.30pm but Mick sometimes kept us out there on Leeds Road Playing Fields until it got dark.

"It was so painful. We'd be out there, standing around, listening and learning, shadow-play, set-pieces. Loads of the lads were moaning – 'Oh my God not again' - but those were the principles which his team was set up on."

He was especially impressed with Buxton's right-hand man, John Haselden.

"If I'd have met John four or five years earlier I'd have been a far better player because he taught me principles and fundamentals of how to defend.

"There were many things like positioning, understanding of the game, when to go and reading of the game and the basics which hadn't been taught. It made me wonder: 'What had I been doing before?'

"We all had our roles and I was mainly a blocker at set-pieces. We scored loads of goals at corners and free-kicks because you couldn't really stop it if you did it well."

According to Hanvey, a 4-1 League Cup hammering by his former colleagues at Grimsby early in the 1979/80 season (when the Mariners won the Third Division title) provided a reality check.

"I went home very annoyed. They were a good team and their attitude was just right. We had to change something at our place.

"There was a lot of soul-searching. I remember saying this is what we've got to aim for – to be a club with a winning mentality.

"We raised our game and I just felt going out there on to the field, looking around thinking no one is going to beat us. There was a tremendous spirit within the camp which built and built."

The Junction pub in Marsh was their destination for a post-match drink after home games on Saturdays and "the order would be something like ten pints of dark mild".

"We were very humble without any edge and if someone wanted to talk football then fine. Everyone would chat to us. We weren't cliquey.

"It's totally different now. It's like a goldfish bowl. But we were normal people, who didn't earn extraordinary money, with a bit of talent for football. We were no better or different to someone with a bit of talent for roofing or decorating."

Like most locals in their 20s or 30s, Johnny's or Flix nightclubs were their ports of call for late nights-out, especially after midweek away games.

"I met my missus, Julie, in Johnny's so I've a lot to blame Huddersfield for.

"I was sat there feeling sorry for myself after a game at Brentford because I'd broken my nose for the umpteenth time.

"I was really down in the dumps because my nose was all over the place and I had black eyes. She reckons my looks have not improved since."

On a more serious note Hanvey ended up being entrusted with the role of Professional Footballers' Association - or players' union - representative and that put him at loggerheads with Buxton.

"I fully respected Mick but we didn't get on because I had to take all the contentious stuff to him – like when we got promoted and I said we want an increase and then he'd come back with 'You're not holding the club to ransom. Get out of here.'

"We were only going in for a fiver or tenner a week extra but that's what he was like. Mick was a dour bugger. He was a clubman and you had to earn your money and that was the way it was."

Hanvey ended up with the union role due to his grammar school education.

"It's sad to say but because I'd I got my O-levels and A-levels, they used to think that I was of a higher intelligence level than most footballers.

"And I probably was in that era because they thought I was one of the only ones who could spell difficult words or write a sentence that was grammatically correct.

"Hardly anyone kept their heads down at school once a career in football beckoned and that's why I was made PFA rep but that just shows how badly educated footballers were if I was a leading light.

"And I even ended up with the nickname 'Bamber' after Bamber Gascoigne who used to present University Challenge."

He was also clever enough to stand up to new signing Steve Kindon.

"Kindo was our marquee signing. It was a bold statement of intent to the fans and also the players.

"Steve could overshadow most people because he was so dominant in the dressing room and not many stood up to him but I did.

"We had a lot of funny moments at each others' expense. We used to do daft things like cutting up underpants. 'Right this is war,' he said, when we sewed up his shirtsleeves.

"Aside from the funny stuff, he made us even more positive. We had to be winners at a time when most of us weren't winners."

Hanvey and his colleagues rose to the challenge in style with that 2-1 win over Hartlepool.

"We never felt pressure and that was to do with the management. When that last game took place, when we had to win, it was just a normal game. There was no added stress.

"It was strange there was a phlegmatic response afterwards in the dressing room. It wasn't a massive relief, thinking we've done it. Phew. It was as if this is what we've trained for.

"This is what we were expected to do. That encapsulates things. But we now know that it lifted Huddersfield Town out of the doldrums. We're proud of that."

After making 235 appearances and scoring 15 goals for Town, Hanvey returned to Rochdale in July 1984 for a season where what he described as a 'one-day contract' meant he could explore the world of business before he head back to Leeds Road as commercial manager.

"I'd gone into sales-repping and was fairly successful at it but I missed the weekends and just felt they were for nothing because in football you built up to something and I was lost for quite a while because of the lack of focus, nothing to play for.

"It was quite a disturbing blow mentally, in my mind, and Steve Kindon recommended me for a job he was vacating at Town and even though I was doing very well in sales, the pull was too much.

"I went back to Huddersfield 18 months after I'd finished and although there were lots of ups and downs, my major contribution to the club was paving the way for the new stadium."

....

Keith Hanvey was ready to kick up a stink in a bid to drive forward the bold plans for a new stadium for Huddersfield.

So he led Town's board of directors to the rancid old toilets behind the terrace in a little tour of the ageing Leeds Road ground.

He did so in his role as the club's commercial manager to persuade chairman Keith Longbottom and his directors that Town had to build a new home but it proved to be a waste of time.

"I thought we needed a new stadium because the club overdraft was going up and I wondered where were we going to go," said Hanvey who lives in Huddersfield and runs his hospitality company, Hanvey Corporate, from home.

"I did all the research on how this sort of thing, moving grounds, had happened at Scunthorpe, where I made countless trips, and St Johnstone and got it to where it was nearly going ahead.

"At one board meeting a week or two before I had a blow-up when the new stadium plans were going to be proposed, I took the directors round to the big main terrace and I took them into the toilet areas and I don't think many of the directors had seen them.

"I said, "have you seen this?' That was my best board meeting – to actually just go out there and look around the ground and see the toilets that were awful but they still said we don't need a new stadium. They were scared and I soon resigned on principle."

Hanvey had been pushing forward the plans to build a new stadium in the face of boardroom opposition and even though he gave up the fight he still left a huge legacy at the club.

"We had a meeting about in principle going ahead but Keith Longbottom and the board turned it down. I had a developer there, I was so into it and put loads of effort into it but in essence we couldn't get it through

"And so in a fit of pique I threw my books on the floor and said 'I'm leaving'. I resigned on the spot. Geoff Headey was my main ally on the board but I told them 'I'm not staying at this club when you've got no ambition.'

"I can't tell you how upset I was when they didn't go ahead with it. It was a four-sided stadium that was practical. It wasn't generally me but I left and amazingly I took all my plans away and threw the toys out of the pram.

"Leaving Town at the point was probably the biggest upset I've had

at Huddersfield Town amid a lot of very good memories. It hurt me badly.

"God knows what could have happened from then because Paul Fletcher took over from me and went on to become a new stadium guru with Bolton and at Wembley and I suppose that could have been me."

Hanvey moved on to Bradford City (and later Leeds United) where he masterminded the building of the big new Valley Parade stand but then received an SOS from new Town chairman Graham Leslie.

"Six months later Graham, who was a good pal of mine, became chairman and he was a very progressive guy and he phoned me up out of the blue at Bradford and asked me back on the promise that we'd get this stadium built. I said 'you're joking me' but he was deadly serious.

"He told me thought the new stadium a fantastic idea and it should happen but I couldn't go back because Bradford had been so good to me and I was working on that big stand behind the goal and it would have been wrong for me to just leave them in the lurch after they'd taken me on.

"He said he was going to go for someone and was going to back him all the way and he went for Paul. He asked if I would give him all my plans and I thought yes I would because you're a good bloke and the rest is history."

Topp draw

Chris Topping

The goalless draw with arch-rivals Bradford City at Valley Parade on November 19, 1979, was one of those games unlikely to live long in the memory but it is one that Chris Topping still relishes.

Topping, who had come to Huddersfield from York City times as a vastly experienced centre-half, was limited to just 13 appearances for Town in the 79/80 season due to the consistency of Dave Sutton and Keith Hanvey.

But when Topping was asked to take centre-stage he never failed to showed why Mick Buxton still describes him as the "ultimate model professional" nearly 40 years after they worked together.

"That Bradford match was one for the purists but only those who like the art of defending," Topping said from his home in Cliffe, near Selby, North Yorkshire.

"It was a tough old game and we really had to dig in but the joy on Mick's face after the final whistle was profound and I immediately felt as though I was part of the squad.

"That meant a lot to me because I had a lot of respect for Mick and he knew that I would never let anyone down, well not intentionally, anyway, and he could trust me enough to bring me in whenever I was needed."

Topping played 378 consecutive games for York and then Huddersfield but accepted his role on the sidelines with grace.

"I wasn't going to say anything against Mick and that wasn't due to fear but because I honestly felt that Mick knew what he was doing.

"I was brought up whereby the boss tells you what to do and you do it. It didn't bother me one little bit that I wasn't chosen and I was there as back-up but that didn't mean I didn't work hard.

"I took it in my stride and trained hard and pushed Keith and Dave as far as I could. That was ideal for Mick because I wasn't crying and I was keeping them on their toes.

"It was always going to be difficult to dislodge Keith because he was good very ball player and Dave was very good in the air and decent on the ground so they were a formidable partnership."

Topping was brought up in Bubwith, near Selby, and worked his way through the local Sunday League and then the Yorkshire League when, at the age of 16, was faced legendary Andy Lochhead.

He became York's first ever apprentice professional and played his first senior game on Boxing Day 1968 but once he got going he became a first-team fixture and from 1969 to 1978 he figured in 355 successive games for York.

That was in an era when local reporter Malcolm Huntington was allowed to travel to away games on the team bus.

Tom Johnson was his manager and he guided the Bootham Crescent club into Division Two for the first time in its history before returning for a second spell with Huddersfield before a ball had kicked a ball in the new season.

York were relegated twice in successive seasons under Wilf McGuinness before Johnson brought Topping - third on the club's all-time appearance list having clocked up 463 games for the Minstermen - to Leeds Road in a £20,000 deal to stem the leaks in Town's defence and even got the York secretary to drive to West Yorkshire.

"Tom was a strange one, a dour Scotsman, a bit of a loner, but I liked him all the same. He wasn't bothered if people liked him or not. He was a real one-off. At York we had a players' revolt over what was happening like dressing room cleanliness and daft things like that.

"He was a penny-pincher. After we'd got promoted to Division 2, one of the best players, Phil Burrows, wanted a £5-rise, when he was worth a lot more. But Tom wouldn't agree so Phil went to Plymouth who were in a lower division."

While Johnston may have been in overall charge he would leave final tactics to his coaches.

"At York, we'd meet at a hotel before games and he'd leave after saying bits and bobs. Then we'd have a proper team-talk with the coach who'd know who we were up against and what tactics we should employ.

"Tom was never going to be a players' manager. He was wonderful at getting players in and knotting a team together for the coaches to work with which is where Mick and John came in. He relied on them to do the football bit.

Topping had not been at Town long when Johnson stepped down.

"Mick and John (Haselden) were left to do all the hard work while Tom sat in his office puffing on his pipe.

"The directors must have read between the lines that Tom was just getting the players, picking the team and once he'd done that he was almost superfluous because it was down to the coaches to do the rest.

"There was a total transformation when Mick took over. He was in charge from Monday morning to Saturday night and he was very good on tactics, especially set-pieces.

"That is where Ian Robins got lots of his goals - free-kicks that were swung in and defenders were blocked by seemingly dozy forwards. It was a great ploy."

Topping continued to be a mainstay of the Huddersfield defence when Buxton took over until a personal calamity struck and his run of games on the spin was abruptly halted.

"We were up against Grimsby (a 2-1 defeat on February 3, 1978) when it was one of the few games not called off due to the weather.

"I went up for ball, came down in the centre circle and tore my cartilage. I went for intensive treatment but my run of consecutive games ended - 23 short of the 401-game record (held by Harold Bell of Tranmere Rovers).

Topping had surgery but when he returned to the fray Hanvey and Sutton were going from strength to strength.

"I was always a team player and I didn't get upset if I wasn't playing but was back-up if either of them got injured or suspended. We had a good team spirit and I always wished them well. They played well together. They looked the part and were the part."

Topping , who went into the market gardening business after retirement, was under no illusions that he was fit for the 1979-80 season as he successfully piggybacked the 6ft 2in, 13-stone Malcolm Brown up the local hills.

"There was a real feeling of togetherness at the club but the biggest lift of all came when Steve Kindon arrived. It was a wonderful atmosphere, joking in the right way about things like the Lancashire-Yorkshire rivalry.

"Steve wasn't there for long but he was my player of the season. He made a huge impact in everything he brought to the club. It was an inspired signing.

"He was funny, he would take a joke, especially about his lisp, and he didn't bother when people were taking mickey out of him. He became the talisman of the club. He made us all feel as though the club must be going somewhere."

It's your time now, Fred.

Fred Robinson

Fred Robinson sensed his chance to take revenge and he wasn't going to miss it.

The Town left-back was ready to get his own back once the number seven board had been hoisted aloft by the Doncaster Rovers coach Les Cocker.

That not only signified that winger Daral Pugh's game was over for the afternoon but it also gave Robinson the chance to have a laugh at former boss Billy Bremner's expense.

Town were winning 3-0 and Robinson could not resist the chance to rub salt into wounds as it was Rovers manager Bremner who had not long since deemed him surplus to requirements at the South Yorkshire club.

"I was near the dugouts and I couldn't resist shouting over at him.

'Eh, Billy.'

'Yeah, what?'

'You looking for Daral?'

'He's here in my pocket.'

"I can't repeat what he said but it was basically along the lines of 'eff off".

"I had a massive smile on my face because Daral getting taken off was the ultimate back-handed compliment."

Robinson certainly had a point to prove because former Leeds skipper Bremner, in his first managerial job, had shown him the door at Doncaster where he had made more than 120 appearances.

"I enjoyed my time at Doncaster till I started having trouble with my knees and then Billy Bremner came in as manager.

"I'd rung Billy up and rightly or wrongly he told me that my knee were knackered which was far from being the case.

"I'd just tried to get back paying after having my cartilages out and I'd played three or four games in a fortnight.

"It was too much too soon and one of the knees was swelling up so it didn't look good."

In a way, Bremner was doing Town a favour as he opted for revolution rather than evolution.

"Billy just wanted a clean sweep, bringing all his own staff and players and I think deep-down – and I know he's not here God bless him – he regretted it afterwards because there were four senior pros he let go.

"I know he wanted to bring young lads in but I knew it was a bad move. There was me, Trevor Phillips who was an England youth international, John Breckin and Alan Crawford

"They'd won the Third Division title 1974/75 and they all went to clubs that got promotion the following season. If only Billy had just sat down and watched us play."

Robinson could easily have ended up on football scrapheap but he wasn't prepared to go down without a fight.

"It hurt like hell when I was let go. At first I was gutted because I knew I still had a lot to offer.

"Mick Hennigan, who was Bremner's assistant, was from our village, and even he said to me, 'Don't be thinking of going into non-league football, no way, you've got a lot more to offer than that.'

"There are always people you meet who say 'when I was younger my mate or my cousin could have made it'. Well what happened? He got released at the age of 15 and started drinking and smoking and was distracted by women. Well there's the answer.

"I didn't throw in the towel but a lot of people do and they fall by the wayside. I just got my head down. I still wanted to play professional football. I was born to be a footballer. It's all I wanted to do.

"Before we played them, I went over to their fans before the game for the kickabout and clapped my hands to them and they did the same in response. So I realised it wasn't the fans that didn't like me which helped me loads.

Robinson kept himself fit playing in a local five-a-side tournament that summer before Buxton cottoned on to the fact that a player he had seen as a youngster was looking for employment.

"I was playing for Rotherham juniors behind a pub one Saturday. I think we beat Scunthorpe 3-1 and I know I scored. That was in the days when I was in the thick of it as a midfielder. It was uncanny.

Robinson regards himself as "unbelievably lucky" that Buxton was there. "That's why I always tell people to play every game as if it's your last because there could be someone watching you.

"After Mick first saw me, I moved into defence because someone got injured and I was asked to fill in at left-back and I never went back to midfield. It was a whole new ball game to me.

"I could at last see everything instead of being in midfield where the ball's always coming over our head. It felt relatively easy being at full-back."

Once he got wind of the fact that Robinson was available, Buxton referred to his scouting notes and gave him the chance to prove himself.

("I saw him for first time playing for Rotherham youth team on a local pitch behind a pub in August in 1973," Buxton said, "and I made mental note: 'He ain't bad.')

"Mick rang me up and I assured him there was nothing wrong with my knees. I told him I'd come and do pre-season training with them. He agreed; we'd take it from there."

Three weeks and a few friendlies later, Robinson was invited into Buxton's office and offered a three-year contract.

"I knew I was fit enough to play so it was just a case of getting in there and working hard to prove myself but I didn't see the three-year contract coming.

"I felt like hugging him but thought better of it. You never got that close to your managers.

"After all the setbacks I'd had, it was unbelievable, especially when we played Doncaster at home."

And then what football writer Brian Glanville called the immutable 'law of the ex' – when footballers have the last laugh on those who got rid of them – was shown to hold good at Leeds Road when they were re-united shortly after going their separate ways.

Robinson was brought up in Thrybergh area of Rotherham, which was something of a hotbed of football talent.

"On that estate, there were the Snodin brothers who lived just around the corner from me and Sheffield United player Alan Ogden and Kenny Boden and went to live in Australia and played for their national team.

"I took the Snodins (Glyn and Ian) to Doncaster when I was in the first team and they were young lads. They were good lads who had really good careers, especially Ian who would have become an England regular if he hadn't got injured when he got into an England squad and never got invited again."

Robinson started playing for his school and earned a place in his town's under-14s schoolboy team and then Yorkshire Boys before signing apprentice forms at Rotherham after a surprise visit.

"I was on the school field, over the fence about 30 yards from our house (Deer Park Road) playing football with my mates, obviously, when I was called back home by my mum.

"She'd shouted my name and I was worried, thinking what's the matter, and she said it was Tommy Docherty. I said 'give over, don't be so stupid, mum'.

"I thought she was winding me up but she wasn't having me on. There he was sat in our house - Tommy Docherty, the Rotherham manager."

Robinson was 15 years old when the future Manchester United manager called in at his house without warning and he was soon packing his bags for his first trip abroad.

'Have you got a passport, son? We're going to Holland next week for ten days for a tournament and I want you to come with us.'

"But the thing was, I didn't have a passport because I hadn't been abroad or anything like that. Foreign travel just wasn't something kids on our estate ever did.

"Anyway, there was a bit of a panic that I was going to miss out. It takes weeks on end now to get a passport so I'd have been shafted these days.

"One thing led to another and next thing I was heading over to the passport office in Liverpool with my uncle who had a motorbike and sidecar so off we went across the Pennines."

And Robinson's career took off in style. "It was under-18s and I was probably the youngest there. That made me grow up quickly. It was fabulous.

"I was in awe of Tommy. He was a man of his word, Tommy was. He promised Rotherham he'd get the club out of this division and he did – we got relegated.

"But, still, Rotherham had a good team at the time and I couldn't get a regular place in the side. I knew it was time to move if I wanted regular first-team football and went to Doncaster."

But it was up the M1 in Huddersfield where Robinson felt most at home.

"We all used to look forward to going into training every day and that's a brilliant feeling.

"People don't always want to go into work but it was the perfect mix of business and pleasure. People don't do their best ever day but us lot, we couldn't wait to go into training even though Mick Buxton worked us really hard.

"Mick was an honest man who knew his football inside-out and if you worked hard for him then you'd get your rewards and he was always firm but fair with us.

"He kept himself to himself to maintain a respectful distance, which made sense. For Mick, familiarity bred contempt and that's why he never got too close to the players."

Buxton clearly rated Robinson and he showed his admiration in the most unflattering of terms.

"He used to call me the 'shithouse rat' because I was always scurrying around, scuffling, getting in between people, being busy. It was a strange kind of compliment.

"There are some people who don't like getting dirty in training but we did and I really did. There were even fights in training. I got sent home from training a few times right throughout my career, even at

Rotherham.

"It was a case of 'Fred, you get back to the ground and sort the tea out for the lads.' You have a practice match and you're up against someone who's keeping you out of the first team and there's no way you're not going to get stuck into him.

"It's a contact sport, after all. That season with Town we weren't so bad. Everyone was on the same wavelength. You get that every now and again as a team. We knew we were onto something special if we worked hard and listened to the manager and coaches and got our heads down."

Robinson had another blast from the past when Town beat Port Vale 7-1 – the most emphatic win since the 1950s.

"They had a centre-half called Bob Delgado who was the captain of the Rotherham team that went up form that bottom division when I was coming through the ranks.

"After the game, Bob – who got taken off - came over to me, shook my hand and said: 'It's your time now Fred.' This was only in October but he knew we had a good side; that we had what it took to get promoted.

"That was a classy touch. Bob even scored an own-goal. We were on fire that day. I shared that with the lads in the dressing room. It confirmed what we were thinking but we weren't blasé about it. We were a hard-working group of players."

A 5-0 win over Northampton also stands out.

"I'd been in bed all day with flu and we were supposed to report in at four o'clock and I can't remember exactly what they gave me – a jab or a bit of medicine – but I was actually laid up on the treatment table until seven o'clock.

"There was no case of 'I can't play because I'm not feeling well' which some people do. Someone woke me up and stuck a bit of Vic up my nose, I came round sharpish and played one of my best ever games."

Robinson played almost every single game until February when he was suspended and Bernard Purdie entered the fray and kept his place until the very end of the season.

"Bernard came in and did a great job. He was a steady pro and I'd have done the same as a manager and left the team as it was because we were winning and Bernard hardly put a foot wrong.

"If I'd been a lot younger, more hotheaded, I'd have probably been upset but I'd gone through a lot and I'd seen people come and go and I just wished Bernard all the best. And why not? We wanted to win that championship.

"It wouldn't have mattered to me whoever had come in if they were doing a better job than me at that time, but come the summer, I told Bernard the gloves are off now because next season is next season.

"I worked my socks off and became first-choice again when we should have gone up again. It's testimony to me that I played 42 games that (1980/81) campaign and I'd have played every one of them if I hadn't got suspended."

Robinson scored just the once during the 1979/80 season, converting a penalty when Crewe were beaten 3-0.

"When people say we scored 101 goals I'll always say I got the 'one' but that was good enough for me.

"I was an out-and-out, old-fashioned defender. I could run and sprint but my job was to defend. If we had a right-winger against us Mick said he knew I'd sort him out.

"I used to look after Dave Cowling as well. If there was any bother he'd just turn round and say 'sort this one out', and he could consider it done but that's also probably the reason my knees are knackered and his are fine."

Robinson also helped Cowling deal with abusive Town fans.

"It was horrible the amount of stick he'd get. But he was a great lad who was blessed with one of the best left feet I've ever seen.

"We all helped him deal with the stick he got from the fans. Some people like you to rally round them and some people like to be left alone but we'd always give him a hug to re-assure him. You'd have a chat with him and he'd be sound. He was a good professional.

"When I finished playing and I was sat in the stand with his family and the fans were having a go. It really upset me because they didn't realise his wife and his children were there and his mum. A lot of it was hurtful; it was nasty."

Town had their ups and downs for much of an ultimately glorious season, but for Robinson the turning point was Steve Kindon's arrival.

"I think we had enough to go up but Steve Kindon added the firepower for us to be champions. He intensified competition for places but he was a big presence off the field as well.

"We welcomed him with open arms. We thought it was a step-up. He'd played top-flight football so he knew what it was all about. He trained hard and quickly established himself as one of the lads.

"He was a seriously funny man. When we had a Christmas do he fell for that old one of us telling him it was fancy-dress and it wasn't and he was the only one to turn up in fancy dress. He saw the funny side."

Kindon and Robinson were both forced to retire from football at the end of the 1980/81 season due to knee injuries, with Robinson snapping a cruciate ligament.

"It was the end of season on a rutted pitch. The caught winger tried to go one way, I turned and he tried to go the other way and my foot stuck and I heard it snap.

"It was excruciating. I'd never experienced pain like it. But then I got up and tried to play on. I didn't know what it was and then all of a sudden I collapsed again. It was like I was back in Johnny's dancing on a bad night. Your feet were stuck to the floor but that didn't do my dancing any harm."

He had 12 months left on his contract when he had to call it a day as knee surgery was still a work in progress.

"The way they treat knees has moved on dramatically. It's a whole new ball game now. We were guinea pigs. It was trial and error. I never got back playing. It wasn't a successful operation.

"We had the best treatment but my knee problems might have had something to do with the grounds we played on or the way I played, without any fear. I never flinched. It's hard to say.

"It was when I started running again I knew it wasn't right. It wouldn't tighten up properly. The bones were crunching. I just knew.

They tried me with cortisone injections and all sorts of things.

"I had to go to Manchester to see if anything could be done. He said it would be impossible to play professional football again so he wrote a letter to the club and that was it. That's when you're gutted – when you know you can't play again."

Things went from bad to worse for Robinson who was ill-prepared to find a new direction in his life beyond football.

"I was totally stunned. Things go through your mind – what do you do now? I wasn't in the right frame of mind at the time. That was probably because of the state of my first marriage. There was drinking and whatever.

"I just couldn't cope with it at first. I was in a bad place. I think probably at that time I was depressed but at that time people in professional sport getting depressed wasn't heard of.

"No one ever talked about sportsmen, professional footballers, getting depressed. Depressed? How can they be depressed? They're professional footballers. You be surprised. But I'd probably had a bit of depression.

"It's commonplace now. People talk about it openly. It's sad that there was such a taboo. Things are so much better now. People are a lot more open these days and more help is available.

"Mixing with old colleagues, getting it off my chest and listening to other points of view helped me get through it, instead of just burying my head in the sand."

Robinson has called Huddersfield home since 1979 and Buxton invited him to work out with senior players after he had retired but he failed to carve out a career in coaching for himself.

"Mick didn't mind me training with them because I was a good trainer. He knew I hadn't come to mess about; that I'd come to help and gee people up. It was silly. I still wanted to be involved. I still went to watch them. I'm still a Town fan now.

"Looking back at that time, when I was in a dark place, I should have just gone and taken all my coaching badges like one or two of my friends have like Dave Sutton, Mark Lillis and Dave Cowling. I've got the first two coaching badges but I wish I'd done it 25 years earlier.

"I worked for the academy for a while as a coach. I think I'm still old school. You've still got to write ten dossiers every day, reports and all this but I just wanted them to play football."

He ended up working in engineering for about 20 years at Huddersfield-based firm Holset and his sporting exploits are now limited to playing golf – sometimes with ex-Town colleagues – at Longley Park Golf Club where he is a member.

He was also there at Wembley when Town won promotion to the Premier League.

"I've never seen so many grown men cry. It was one of the best days of my life. Emotion-wise it was unbelievable. It sounds daft but thinking about that game now sends a shiver right down my spine."

....

Fred Robinson not only helped Town to silverware but he also helped Almondbury United win the Huddersfield and District Football League.

"Ian Gibson, who I knew from our days at Town, picked me up from my house for a game against Lindley Working Men's Club for our first match at Almondbury Rec.

"I didn't know where the pitch was. There were kids swinging on goalposts and there were bricks and glass all over the place. I said 'so where's the pitch?'

"He said that's it. We're not playing on that are we? It was unbelievable. But that was it – welcome to the real world Mister Robinson.

"We did well even though we played on a pitch that sloped so much I asked the manager if he had a bit of lead that I could stick in my ear to help me balance.

"And our centre-half, Wally, could through the ball from the sidelines into the goalmouth. It was like a corner.

"I got a bit of stick from the opposition but I just mixed in with my team-mates so we all got on well. They expected me to turn up and be a prima donna but that's not in my nature.

"I just got stuck in, I wanted to win. I could hardly run but I still had it upstairs so I didn't need to run. I really enjoyed it that season but I couldn't go any further. I'd be in a wheelchair now if I'd carried on."

Leader of the pack

David Blakeley

It was the stuff that diehard football fans' dreams are made of.

Lifelong Town supporter David Blakeley travelled throughout England watching the Terriers in action – and then became an honorary member of the first team squad.

It was thanks to his loyalty that Dave became a familiar face to Mick Buxton and then, out of the blue (and white), he received an invitation to really get stuck in.

"I followed them all over the place and ended up getting to know Mick Buxton," said David.

"I first had a word with him in 1978 when he was getting a bit of stick but I'd always said: 'Give the man a chance'.

"He knew I was fanatical and then he made me an offer I couldn't refuse when we were chatting.

'Why don't you come and have a kickabout with us?'

"It was like all my Christmases and birthdays rolled into one. When I told my mates they said: 'Oh aye, and pigs might fly, too.'"

The players took him to their hearts and nicknamed him Johnny Mathis because of his passing resemblance to the black American singer.

"I was super-fit in those days so I joined them on cross-country runs. I could run all over the place, uphill and down dale, and I led the way.

"One day we were running along the canal and Steve Kindon got sick of me being in the front all the time and threw me into the canal.

"The trouble was I couldn't swim so I started panicking. I was in a right state. I was flapping around. They were all laughing because it was the sort of thing they did to people on their birthdays.

"I shouted out to them that I couldn't swim and they suddenly stopped when they realised I was in danger of drowning. Dave Sutton came to my rescue. He jumped in and fished me out. It was one of those jokes that went wrong."

Dave, who used to work in the textile industry and is now a Kirklees Council road-sweeper, used to dodge lorries as he cycled along the A62 Leeds Road for training.

"I walked into the changing rooms and no one was bothered. It was always: 'Hiya Johnny.'

"I'd be there in the mornings when they concentrated on fitness with running and weights, we'd do a bit of ball work and then have a bit of food. I also got to play.

"One day Andy Rankin didn't turn up because he was poorly and so Mick turned to me and said 'Johnny, will you go in goal for the second team?' I did all right. I even saved a penalty from Steve Kindon.

"The players all really took to me. They were so nice to me on and off the field and I keep I touch with them now and they still call me Johnny."

People came and went but 'Johnny' became a first-team fixture.

"I was getting changed next to Micky Kennedy and a coach came in, counting the players.

'Who's this?'

'Who are you?'

'Never mind who am I, what are you doing here?'

'I'm a supporter and I always come and train with the players.'

"They didn't mind. They let me carry on.

"I even turned up for training on Christmas Day. 'You're keen you,' one of them said. Too right I was. They were like a family to me."

Do or die

Mick Buxton

Mick Buxton sat down at his desk in the Town manager's office.

He flicked through his Rolodex for the number of Halifax Town counterpart Jimmy Lawson and reached for the telephone.

Still reeling from seeing his team lose 3-2 at Hereford despite leading through two goals from striker Bobby Campbell, Buxton was poised to take decisive action.

'Jimmy? Mick Buxton here. Bobby Campbell? Do you want him?'

'Eh?'

'Bobby Campbell. Do you want him?'

'How much?'

'You can have him.'

'Bobby Campbell? Really?

'Aye. But there's one condition - you've got to sign him by lunchtime, I'll tell you now, so get yourself over here now. He'll be here waiting for you, and sign him.'

Buxton summoned Campbell to his office.

'Sit down Bobby..... Bobby you're leaving.'

'What? You're joking.'

'You're leaving Bobby. You're going. You're going to Halifax today.'

'No I'm not. I'm not going to Halifax. I like it here now. I'm staying.'

'Bobby. You're not stopping here. I'll spell it out to you now. You are leaving. You are going to Halifax Town. Jimmy Lawson is coming over to see you.'

'I'll go training at 10.15am and when I get back, you make sure that you have signed for Halifax Town.'

'Ah, you're bloody joking. You don't scare me.'

'Bobby I'm not trying to scare you. I'm telling you the truth, the facts. When I come back from training, you make sure you have signed for Halifax Town.'

'But I'm not going anywhere. I've got a two-year contract. I've just signed it.'

'I know you have but you'll not get anything because every time you step out of line, I'm going to fine you and I'm going to take all your bloody money off you.'

'Arrgh. You don't scare me.'

'I'm telling you I am not trying to scare you. I'm just telling you how it's going to be. Right?'

'So I'm going now Bob. You can sit here if you want but I'm going bloody training. When I come back make sure you've signed for Halifax Town.'

"And that was him gone."

That was Buxton's reaction to defeat against a Hereford side featuring future Wimbledon manager Bobby Gould who led the Crazy Gang to FA Cup glory against Liverpool.

"He'd already been at Huddersfield in the past and everyone thought what a good player Bobby Campbell is.

"He'd been in America and he'd come back. We were short of players and the directors were on about signing Bobby Campbell.

"I was trying to pull things together and put things right and they signed him. It was their doing.

"To be honest, I'd had him about a week and I was fed up with him. 'Oh, I thought, I can't have this.'

"He wanted to take everything over, Bobby. He talked in a gruff, loud voice all the time. He wanted to be in charge of everything."

Buxton's mind was made up by that Hereford game.

"We were winning 2-0 at half time and ended up losing 3-2. He'd packed in at half-time. He'd scored two goals and then packed in.

"Anyhow, next morning I called Jimmy, who had played for Huddersfield and was a really nice fella, because I knew he wanted him and Bobby was on his way."

For Buxton their parting of the ways was crucial to his own well-being.

"There are big decisions in your life and this was a big decision I had to make. He had to go.

"That was very important because if I hadn't done that I'd have lost the dressing room. I'd have lost everything. I'd have been dead. Everything would have fallen apart.

"Some players would say 'well I've got my wife and kids' to me. 'So do you think I live on my own?'

"At the end of the day, I've got a family and I've got to feed them and you're not going to get in my way. There is a cut-off point.

"That was a big thing. He thought he was the big lad and then the players look at that and think hang on a minute, if I step out of line here, the same thing could happen to me.

"Could sports psychologists do what I did? No. They couldn't because they've never played football or been in football before."

....

The long and the short of it is that Tom Johnston and Mick Buxton did not see eye-to-eye on quite a few things including what it took to be a good footballer.

"If you weren't 6ft 3in Tom didn't like you - you had to be a giant to get in his team," Buxton said.

"When I first arrived there were six centre-halves and one of them, Keith Hanvey, was playing outside left because he was left-footed. How the hell did that come about?

"One night he told me to watch Nottingham Forest reserves against Manchester City reserves and Asa Hartford was playing. I came back and went to his office and he's there smoking his pipe with the papers in front of him looking at the horseracing.

"He asked me how he's done with his pipe in his mouth and he's done well but when I told him he was only about 5ft 7in he muttered 'that's not good is it?'

"That was the last we heard of him because he wasn't good enough for Tom because he was 5ft 7in and then he went on to become a hero at Manchester City and played in the World Cup finals for Scotland."

From zero to hero

Brian Stanton

Brian Stanton was just about to head for home when there was a tap on his shoulder from a stranger.

It was while he was getting to his feet in the main stand at Leeds Road that he was asked by a member of the club staff to go downstairs for a word with Town manager Mick Buxton.

He was soon on his way to Buxton's office, moments after the referee's whistle put had put Town out of their misery at the end of a 4-1 defeat by Grimsby at Leeds Road.

Stanton had been sat with a Bury colleague to size up his prospective new teammates at the behest of Buxton who had seen Town suffer the club's worst defeat at Leeds Road in 12 years in the second leg of their League Cup tie.

Buxton clearly had cause for concern but was not fearful about his own job security or Town's promotion prospects following a reality check by the Mariners who had just won gone up from the Fourth Division.

Instead, he was anxious that Stanton, a player he was trying to tempt to drop down a division and join Town, might head back over the Pennines and never come back.

"It showed Mick was clearly keen to stop me in my tracks but he needed haven't bothered," Stanton said over a beer at Manchester's Football Museum.

"He made it clear that he wanted to sign me but knew I was unsure so he'd invited me over and I got a lift with my Bury team-mate, Jimmy McIlwraith, who drove me over because I didn't have a car.

"Even though we watched Town getting a right stuffing, me and Jimmy both felt they were not a bad side but they were getting punished for everything by a hell of a good side.

"I liked the way Town wanted to play, from the back and through midfield and the atmosphere was brilliant despite the result.

"As soon as the match ended, I was hastily summoned into the gaffer's office. Someone tapped me on the shoulder and said the manager wanted to see me straight away.

"I went down to see him and he was all apologetic, 'We're not that bad. Don't read too much into this, it was an off-day, they're a really good side and they were the best side in our division last year.'

"I nodded in agreement but it didn't matter because I'd made my mind up. I thought I fancy this. I could fit in and within ten days I signed (for £13,500) and I didn't regret it one bit."

After playing 41 games on the spin in his maiden season, Stanton went on to make a total of 241 appearances and score 54 goals for Town before leaving in 1986 and ending his career as a full-back at Rochdale and re-training as a joiner.

That which wasn't bad going for someone once not deemed good enough to represent his Merseyside school at football.

"It was strange because when I was about 15, I couldn't get in the school team. That's because at the time, there were so many good players there (at St Kevin's Comprehensive School).

"It bugged me because I thought I was good enough for the school team. I could run all day which was an asset but at the age of 15/16 people shot above me."

Despite the setback, nothing that happened at school could put Stanton off pursuing his goals ("Most kids from my generation dreamed of being an astronaut or a footballer.")

"We were about 15, and our headmaster stood up, talking about careers and said: 'I know everyone here will want to be a professional footballer, but let me tell you now, that's not going to happen to any of you.'

"He told us not to be dreamers. He'd be right 99 times out of 100 but on that occasion he was wrong – twice. It ended happening to two of us, me and a lad called Joe Hinnigan who played for Wigan and Sunderland.

"There were lots of kids who'd had a chance. They were on the local clubs' books and they meant I couldn't get a look in but in the end a lot of them had got nowhere and didn't even play local football which was a shame.

"When I started playing in local leagues, they felt they'd been let down and released and couldn't take it. It also said a lot about them in that they didn't have the hunger to want to play.

"That lack of desire might have been one of their failings. But I stuck at it because I just loved football and wanted to play and I didn't care whether anyone thought I was good or not. I just loved doing it."

Into his late teens, Stanton, who was brought up in Kirby, continued to have an insatiable appetite for football that kept him on track.

"I used to bug my mates because when they were going out, I'd go training by myself three times a week to the local sports centre.

"I was on the athletics track running, running up the cycling track ramps, doing my own routines with the ball, anything to tick over. And right next to it were five-a-side pitches and I'd get invited to have a game of footy."

Stanton's boyish enthusiasm for football paid off and led him to join Bury.

"When I was about 18 my sister's boyfriend asked me to play for his pub team, The Oyster, but that didn't go too well at first. I was rubbish because I didn't know any of the players.

"They had a right laugh at my expense because the lads were saying 'Peter, who on earth have you brought us? You're having a laugh with this lad.' But they stuck with me and accepted me and I think I got player of the year.

"I got lucky and it worked out. One of the lads' friends was on Bury's books and he came home at weekends to see his mum and dad and mates and watched us. He'd heard Bury were looking for players so put my name forward. He got me through the door."

So Stanton joined Bury on trial and impressed them enough to be asked, in November 1975, to consider signing on a temporary basis at Gigg Lane to the end of the season.

"I turned it down because I wanted to finish my engineering apprenticeship the following February and that was my priority.

"I told them: 'You might get rid of me and then I've got nothing to fall back on.'

"Luckily enough, as well as keeping machines ticking over as a maintenance fitter in a factory, I played in the reserves. It went well and so on March 1, 1976, I was signed and promptly took a 50 per cent wage cut to play football on £35 a week."

Opportunities were restricted because there was only one substitute in those days but Stanton worked his way into the first team.

"The former Sunderland manager, Bob Stokoe, came in and luckily enough he liked me and encouraged me like mad. He was really complimentary which was good for my self-esteem.

"It was looking good and I did well but then Bob left and Dave Hatton took over as player-manager in May 1978 but he didn't take to me.

"I wasn't in the running at all. I couldn't understand it at all. Maybe it was me thinking I was better than I was but I had belief in myself.

"At the start of the 1979/80 season, I wasn't even involved in the pre-season warm-up games and the writing was on the wall. So after the first few weeks, I had a word with him and told him I was unhappy and it was no good me being here.

"I'd only been in the game a few years and I wanted to do something. So I asked for a transfer. I had nothing to lose; I'd got a contract till the end of the season so I was hopeful something would happen."

Within two weeks, Hatton told him Huddersfield had made contact, wanting a chat with his restless young player.

"At first I had thought: 'Oh, Huddersfield Town? Fourth Division? Do I really want to go down a division? I don't know. Shall I hang on and wait to see if anyone else is interested?

"There was lots of doubt in my mind. But I knew Malcolm Brown and Ian Robins, who were at Town, from Bury and I had a chat with them, which almost made my mind up.

"They said in the last 12 months Town had been a club transformed. Things were happening. Something big was about to take place.

"Mally said there was no comparison between when he arrived with

Stanton was on his way and so, eventually was Hatton who was sacked two months after Stanton's departure, replaced by reserves coach Dave Connor who had tried to persuade the midfielder to "stay put because things were going to change soon".

It was too little, too late and so, ten days after the Grimsby game, Stanton joined Town on Monday, September 1979.

He doubled his basic wage to £70 a week but still had to rely on getting lifts to training each morning.

"The Lancashire contingent would meet at meet at junction 17 of the M62 and jump in one car but I had to get the bus to the meeting point.

"It was well worth it. We got to know each other very quickly because of the travelling arrangements.

"If you said a word out of place, they'd jump on it and you'd get ripped to bits. You had to take it and give it back when you got your chance."

Stanton hit the ground running and "instantly got the crowd on my side" after being propelled from Bury's reserves into Town's first team.

He scored what the *Huddersfield Daily Examiner* described as a "tremendous goal" in his first game, a 1-1 draw at Scunthorpe on the Friday night, before scoring on his home debut in the 7-1 demolition of Port Vale.

"The manager gave us a rollicking at half-time. We dominated, and let them score and he said that might make a big difference in terms of goal difference. It might have seemed petty but it enforced the fact that you can't rest on your laurels.

"Yes it was curmudgeonly but it's only in looking back afterwards that it was his mentality – you punish a team by putting goals in and not having any sympathy.

"That was bit trickier for me because in the Port Vale team was Peter Farrell. I played with Peter at Bury and I was still in digs with him in Bury. He got a fair bit of ribbing."

Town got motoring and Stanton treated himself to a car – a second-hand Ford Escort – but continued to rent a flat in Bury, only buying his first house in his second season with Town.

While he scored nine goals in his debut season – including his first ever hat-trick in senior football in a 5-0 win at home against Stockport - it was also Stanton's work ethic that ensured he was preferred to the arguably more skilful Ian Holmes.

"I was the link-up man between defence and attack down the right wing so we could get the best out of Malcolm Brown. The way we were to play, the manager wanted to utilise Mally to maximum effect because he'd cause havoc and there's no doubt he did. He was brilliant.

"We had a very fit team and that would get you at least half a dozen points. Training was hard and at times brutal.

"A lot of it was down to shuttles or doggies as we called them because you'd end up throwing up like a dog. It was like the early onset of the beep test. We'd be up and down Kilner Bank, long-distance and then short stuff, piggybacks,

"But it paid dividends because we were resilient and we never gave up. That was best illustrated by the fact that when we drew 1-1 with Walsall towards the end of the season the reporter, Stan Solomons wrote us off.

"I remember him saying: 'The draw virtually kills off Huddersfield's chances of the championship.' That was the only point we dropped in our last eight games."

It must have helped that Stanton and his colleagues were as well behaved off the field as they were on it.

"We did everything in moderation. We didn't even drink because we had to drive home and there was no drinking if we had a mid-week game. We were disciplined. We knew how to have a good time as well but we weren't going to abuse things.

"We played card games on the way to away games but we weren't allowed to bet and no money changed hands. It would have got out of control. It would've caused problems between individuals."

Steve Kindon had the odd cigarette and, according to Stanton the goalkeepers, Alan Starling and Andy Rankin, smoked "probably because they got bored because we were so good and they had nothing else to do".

Stanton, who sported children's size five-and-a-half Puma boots, which carried no VAT so were more affordable, had an immaculate disciplinary record.

"I never got booked in all my time at Huddersfield but I wasn't ever scared to get stuck in. Gary Lineker was never booked but he never tackled anyone. For me, timing was everything – but it always helped if you had a nice word with the referee."

As well as buttering up referees, Stanton and his colleagues enjoyed chatting with Town supporters.

"There were times you loved the adulation and you got your ego boosted like mad, especially after a 7-1 win. But you didn't feel superior to anyone. When we were playing, it was just what you wanted to do.

"We always used to call in at The Junction on the way back home and it was always packed with supporters. We'd have a couple of shandies and a bit of craic with the fans. There were lots of familiar faces and you'd chat with them and others asking for autographs.

"Imagine it now, there'd be selfies left, right and centre, it would be chaos. Social media has a lot to answer for. It's such a shame because it means players lose touch with fans.

"Back then there was no grief. It was very amiable. It brought the players and fans closer because it built rapport. It would be those Junction regulars, when you're having a stinker and getting grief, who'd be the ones that would stick up for you.

"There was one lad who put his money where his mouth was. He came up to me in the pub. 'Sign your name on my arm, will you?' I thought it was pointless but he said tomorrow I'm going to get that tattooed on. Two weeks later I bumped into him and there was his 'Brian Stanton' tattoo. It was absolutely barmy."

....

Brian Stanton is a heroic figure in more ways than one.

He will always be remembered for his role in Town's Fourth Division title-winning side.

And his four goals when Town beat Bradford City 6-3 as the Terriers rose to the second tier of English football confirmed his place in local folklore.

But even by his standards, what Stanton has done since is special because three years ago he donated one of his kidneys to his wife of more than 30 years, Angela.

It was after Angela, a lawyer, developed a kidney problem and medics diagnosed her with a rare autoimmune disease that Brian stepped up to the mark when it emerged she needed a transplant.

"It one of the most important things I've done in my whole life because it made a massive difference to the most important person in my life," said Stanton who is a housing officer at Bolton Council.

"When I had tests after Angela was ill it became clear I was almost a perfect match for her so I had no hesitation about donation. We went into hospital together and so there were stresses and strains on our three kids who were frightened.

"After the operation you feel as though you've just been kicked in the stomach by a horse, but that goes after a few days and the long-term benefits far outweigh a bit of discomfort.

"It was an incredible experience but the good thing now is that if I forget our anniversary I'm forgiven."

Wags

They say behind every great man is a great woman and that would appear to be the case judging by these three female perspectives on life in and around Huddersfield Town.

Maureen Buxton

Mick and me met at the Mecca dance hall in Burnley and were married 53 years ago when I was 19 and he was 20.

While he's been in management, we've been to a lot of clubs but Huddersfield was by far the outstanding one and our best days were there.

It was the people and the way the team played and seemed to respect everything Mick said to them. It was a special feeling to go there on a Saturday to a match. It felt like home.

I went to nearly every game and I looked forward to all of them. I loved the excitement.

I'd sit in the stand and enjoy the banter with the fans and try my best to keep my mouth shut if anyone said anything wrong about Mick.

Mick would go out first thing in the morning and not come back till nine or ten o'clock at night. He'd have done his training and then gone out to watch a game somewhere.

He did all his own scouting for players and looking at teams they were about to play. I didn't see a right lot of him. I just kept things steady at home and carried on as best I could.

Mick was easy to live with most of the time but could be hard to live with if things hadn't gone well on the pitch. I didn't talk about things that had gone wrong. I didn't understand tactics. All I could see was a goal going in.

We've got two sons. One was a Barnsley supporter, which I think was because they got a lot of stick at school because they were local rivals. If you can't beat them join them and so he used to go all over watching Barnsley.

Jacqueline Sutton

I still don't know whether to laugh or cry when I think back to that place they put us up above the club shop.

I remember Dave saying 'she can't stay there' and so they put us up in bed-and-breakfast to the end of the season. It wasn't the best of places but there was only the two of us so it didn't really matter.

In November 1979 we had our first child so there were a lot of changes in our lives but David was settled, he liked the club and the football became our social life because I didn't know anybody but I love the game so that was fine.

It was difficult to make ends meet when we bought our first house which was at Dewsbury Moor. I was three months pregnant when we moved in and we just about managed the deposit. We were both only 21 and mortgage rate was sky-high.

You're talking about one percent now but it was 11 or 12 per cent back then and it jumped up again just afterwards. We didn't have much money but there was just enough to get by.

We weren't in debt or anything. I used to work in a bank so I kept a close eye on the money. Everything was accounted for.

I didn't think they were being ripped off. A club has to live within its means so they can only pay what they can afford to pay. Whatever you earn you want to earn a bit more and because they were doing so well they'd get win bonuses which helped.

But we didn't have holidays and we didn't go out for meals so our social life was the football. I was proud to watch David and the team and I'd take the baby with me to matches.

There was the players' lounge and I could use the toilet there so we didn't have to use the normal facilities in the ground. There were no baby-changing facilities, but there was a sink and then a little area where I could lie her down and change her nappy if needs-be and sit down if had to top her up.

There wasn't a lot of money but they were good times. We were happy with what we had, he enjoyed the football, I enjoyed the football and we had our baby and we were happy. That's all we needed.

Janet Laverick

We got married in 1975 and we moved down to Southend when I was 21 and in those days it was a big thing to move away from home.

We had a phone but neither of our parents had phones so keeping in touch was hard and I remember my mum having to ring us from a phone box.

The first thing we did was learn to drive, Mick got a car, and our mums had phones installed so we could keep in touch.

If the football hadn't gone well, Mick wasn't grumpy but he'd be quiet, especially if he'd not done very well himself.

If he was quiet I knew to leave him alone and he'd come through it himself. They need to think things through, replaying every pass in their mind.

We certainly didn't live the high life but then again when Mick moved to Huddersfield our eldest was just a few months old so there was hardly any chance of that happening because I was at home looking after the baby and then we had our second in 1981 when Mick was there.

When we lived in Mansfield, because we're local it wasn't 'wow, there's Mick Laverick.' It was just Mick's job.

He went to work, did his training and then played matches on Saturdays. Because our kids were so small I was wrapped in that side of life rather than the football but I wished they'd been old enough to see him play for Town.

Outstanding to outsider

Ian Holmes

Ian Holmes can pinpoint the exact point when he ran out of steam and his journey with Town took a turn for the worse.

The attacking midfielder began the 1979/80 season with a starting slot in Mick Buxton's team and was set to build on promise shown in the previous campaign.

Holmes underlined his potential by slotting home a penalty in a 3-0 win over Doncaster at Leeds Road but fell out of favour with the unforgiving Buxton following a surprise defeat by Lincoln City.

"We played at Grimsby in a League Cup game on a Wednesday," said Holmes. "We were losing one-nil and I ran myself into the ground thinking if we keep it at 1-0, which we did, we've got a chance in the second leg.

"Then on the Saturday we played Lincoln City away at Sincil Bank. Mick Buxton was ill and so John Haselden took charge. We lost 2-0 which was a bit of a shock.

"I'll never forget that game. My legs had gone. I was absolutely dead and the team was dead from the Grimsby game. We'd played and tried that hard.

"We were running on empty right from the word go. My legs felt hollow. I had nothing. You'd put it down to just having a bad game but now you'd obviously know what was wrong.

"But something happened between me and the coach. Mick got on to me and two weeks later they bought someone else (Brian Stanton) which was a bit sad for me although it was a brilliant season.

"It pissed me off a bit that I couldn't get in the team but when they're winning virtually every week you can't go into the manager's office demanding to know why you weren't getting a game."

Holmes had been signed by Buxton's predecessor Tom Johnston

and got off to a decent start following a change of management and scored 11 goals in 31 games in the 1978/79 campaign.

"I really enjoyed that season. It just clicked. We were playing catch-up because it had been a really bad winter and we'd had lots of postponements but when we got going there was no stopping us. The nucleus of the team that got us up from third-bottom to ninth was the one that got us promoted."

Town were on the up but Holmes says, somewhat cryptically, that he "got on the wrong side of one or two people".

According to Buxton, Stanton was only brought in after he held showdown talks with Holmes.

"I sat down with Holmesie and told him in no uncertain terms I wanted more effort, more running up and down the wing, to make the team work but he said that wasn't his game so I brought someone else in."

Holmes became a fringe player but still scored three goals in his ten games that season as Stanton made the berth on the right side of midfield his own but he was still laughing all the way to the bank.

"I had a good deal at Huddersfield. I'd been on quite good money at York with being one of the better players and Tom managed to get me a £1,500 loyalty bonus each year at Town.

"It was the mid-70s and I was getting £1,500 a year for just stopping at Huddersfield, which was brilliant. The first time I got it, I thought 'bloody hell, something's wrong,' but then I looked at my contract and there it was. I think that was one of the reasons they got rid of me."

Holmes began his professional career in style, when he played for Sheffield United against a star-studded Manchester United team at Old Trafford.

"It was 21-year-old me and people like George Best, Bobby Charlton and Denis Law on the other side of the pitch.

"George Best was my schoolboy hero so I suppose you could say it was downhill from there on.

"I look back and I think 'you did some great stuff so don't worry' but I do beat myself up sometimes for not really being professional.

That's the key word.

"I look back and think 'bloody hell, you should have tried harder' but when you're in your 20s you don't see it."

Holmes was vying for a place at Sheffield United with Bramall Lane hero Tony Currie so becoming a regular in the Blades first team was always going to be a tall order.

He left and helped York City reached the old Second Division for the first time in the club's history under Johnston and did his bit with Town so there is plenty to be proud of but he still looks back with regret.

"I actually do believe that I really under-achieved. You could say I was a luxury player in a way but I was the one who could create the goals and score the goals.

"So I didn't think I had to do a lot of running which meant I didn't run or work as much as hard as I should have done.

"I was quite happy at York and Huddersfield when they were doing well. But I probably didn't have that killer instinct.

"I don't know for sure but that was probably why I didn't make it as a top-class pro."

Holmes was snapped up on a free transfer by Johnston in his days as York manager and he lived life to the full.

"It was brilliant being a footballer. Even when you'd had a bad game the day before, you'd wake up with a fantastic feeling that you were going to work. And that was without the money they get now.

"I know the '70s were different and that there was more of a drinking culture and so I wasn't really by myself on that one. I used to drink a lot but I didn't drink any more than anyone else.

"When you've got midweek games, they say it takes 48 hours for your nervous system to settle down and get back to normal after playing a football game in front of a crowd. So you had to go out.

"For me it was part-and-parcel of football – going out with the lads and getting drunk and having a blow-out because nine times out of ten you were off the next day and then the following day you'd train it away.

"It was especially the case at York where I had quite a few football mates and we used to go out drinking a lot. We were professional enough not to go out Thursday and Friday – although I knew some people who used to but that's a different story.

"But Monday, Tuesday and Wednesday were all right if we didn't have a midweek game. Being single and very athletic you go down that road a bit as it were. I was both feet, straight in. And why not?"

It could have worked out differently for Holmes, he reckons, had he found domestic bliss and settled down sooner rather than later.

"I didn't get married until I was in my mid-30s but I've got no excuse. Not everybody else was doing it but there were quite a few.

"I sometimes wonder if I'd got married when I was in my mid-20s when I was serious with a girl, whether things might have turned out different with someone to calm me down a bit.

"We've all got regrets. You can look back and think if I'd done this or done that then who knows what might have happened but touch-wood I've still got two arms and two legs, a beautiful daughter and some super grandkids."

Despite the questionable re-fuelling habits, Holmes helped York reach the old Second Division and stay there for two seasons that have cemented his place in club folklore along with Johnston.

"Tom was a good old Scottish guy. He was a good psychologist. He seemed to know which buttons to press for me.

"His man-management was good, he made you want to play for him and I had a lot of respect for him. He knew what he was up to football-wise but tactically he wasn't really up to much.

"I hit it off with Tom and we got promoted into second tier but he was not given enough money to bring in new players and strengthen us. He left and then two years later he came back to get me which was a compliment."

After leaving Town, Holmes, who is now 66 and drives a taxi for a living around South Yorkshire, hooked up with Neil Warnock who talked him into moving out of the Football League and going to Gainsborough.

"I knew Neil was going to make it with such a gift of the gab. He's

Marmite. You either love him or hate him but we had some great times together. I told him he'd make it and he said: 'Me and you, we'll go to the top together.'"

"He fell out with Gainsborough and I stuck with them till the end of the season but promised I'd join him at Burton which I did. He said 'I've been worried sick, I've been telling my wife that Ian's not going to join me' which was very flattering.

"Neil was great with me at Burton but I just didn't feel welcome there. I had a bad back and they were supposed to be paying me £60 a week but they weren't coming forward with that so I had to keep ringing them. But I just didn't feel right so I drifted out of football."

Holmes points to that as the time he "was starting to break up" but parting ways with Warnock helped him fall back in love with the game with Wathe Saracens.

"At the end of year, Neil said I've got you a deal at Norton Woodseats or wherever and I just said Neil I'm not bothered – I just want to play with my mates which I did and I had ten great years.

"In football, you can get people that you don't really like who bugger off and do their own thing. But we were all mates, living in a little village and with us winning every week it was great.

"You had to look after yourself but that was part of the fun and anyway our team were like chuffing warriors. I didn't have to worry about anyone kicking me or anything because there were five or six in that team that no one would mess with.

"The legendary hardman, Billy Whitehurst, came from the next village to me and believe you-me, he wasn't the only one like that in those parts and they were playing Sunday League.

"I'd never have thought I could do anything like playing Sunday League football after playing professional football but it was brilliant. The camaraderie was brilliant. It's what kept me going. It really did."

He prospered when he wore a football kit but found the going harder when he was suited and booted.

"A couple of my football mates persuaded me to go into the financial trade but being a financial adviser just didn't suit me at all. I had a couple of years doing that but it actually set me on the wrong path.

"Selling is a gift and I just haven't got it. They used to talk about 'closing people'. You'd go round people's houses getting them to sign on the dotted line so it didn't suit me.

"I was also a croupier for a while at casino in Sheffield. We went to a poker school but I'd been there at the casino a few weeks later the place burnt down."

Holmes faced an altogether new challenge as he struggled to settle into the rhythms of life without football.

"I sank into a depression quite a lot. You do. You don't realise when you've been in football from 14 years old to 31 when everything is taken care of and your life is regimented.

"It's a case of 'do this, do that, be here at ten o'clock' and in between – well I shouldn't say this - have a good time as well. I didn't realise what was wrong with me to start with. I was thinking: "What's the matter with me, what's the matter with me?'

"But in my mid-40s, it finally came out. I wasn't sleeping. In fact for two weeks I didn't sleep once. I didn't have a minute's sleep and it came out that I was depressed from football.

"I got no help at all then but thankfully there is a lot more support available now. Everybody recognises it and they look out for signs of depression.

"I fell into taxi driving because I couldn't handle working in a factory and being stuck inside all day. It's more easy-going and it suited me so I stuck with it."

·····························

John Haselden clearly got up Ian Holmes' nose in more ways than one, according to Mick Buxton.

"As well as being a hard taskmaster, John used to make his own smelling salts, which he'd give to the players before they went out to play," said Buxton.

"But once before a game Ian more or less staggered back into the

dressing room and sat down. I looked at him and thought he might have had a bloody heart attack.

"What the hell's up? It took him an age to come to his senses. The team was waiting to go out and he eventually got to the point where he could talk it was: 'Who did that?' he asked us. 'Who did what?

"Instead of just having a little whiff, Holmesie had a really good go and it had nearly knocked his head off. What had happened wasn't funny but you don't get any sympathy from any player or staff. Nobody said sorry or anything like that."

The man they loved to hate

Dave Cowling

It was supposed to be a pleasant occasion when Dave Cowling and a few of his Town teammates had made their way to the Colne Valley social club.

They were, after all, there to smile, sign autographs, have photographs taken with Town fans and generally talk all things football.

It was one of those nights when nothing could go wrong thanks to the feel-good factor created across Huddersfield by Mick Buxton's players.

But things took an astonishingly snide turn for the worse due to the fact that Cowling had become the player that Town fans – even the youngest ones – loved to hate.

"You'd get split into different groups to do functions and I went with three of the lads to Linthwaite Working Men's Club or something like that.

"We'd gone in and been introduced to everyone and then I was sat down signing autographs with a couple of other lads and this young kid came over.

'All right lad? Give us your pen.'

'No you're all right, I don't want your autograph, my dad says you're shite.'

"You think to yourself: 'Do I really want to be here, hearing this?' The answer was 'no'."

That strange sense of loathing was probably down to a couple of factors.

For starters, Cowling was not really one for the full-blooded 50-50 challenges that people like full-back Fred Robinson used to relish and which get fans' juices flowing.

But also Cowling had not one but two tough acts to follow, handed the No9 shirt instead of the combative and hugely popular Bobby Campbell before becoming the long-term replacement for fans' favourite Kevin Johnson down the left flank.

"To start off with, in the first month or so, I thought the fans had taken to me quite well. Then I started to get absolutely shocking abuse.

"The season we got promoted I always remember one game in particular. I was running down the line, a lad tackled me and the ball ran out of play.

"As I went to pick the ball up one of the fans leant over the fence and said 'Cowling, I'll give you a tenner if you leave.'

"I thought thanks for that. That's absolutely great. I had a lot to put up with. I got dog's abuse."

No matter how well Cowling did, there seemed to be no escape from the bile.

"We'd beaten someone about 4-0 and I'd scored one and made a couple. I remember leaving the ground out of the main exit and walking towards my car and my family.

"I was behind two fellas and I overheard one of them say, 'That was an absolutely great game, Town played really well, but it's a pity about Cowling scoring because that means he'll be playing next week'.

"I know Fred confronted a few of the big-mouthed fans but I learned to hit back. One shouted to me when I was taking a corner 'Who's fucking your wife while you're here?' and I just turned round and said 'Well it's not you, you fucking ugly bastard.' I was getting older and wiser."

Still, it got to the point where Cowling, a key team member of Mick Buxton's team and the scorer of some of the most memorable goals in Leeds Road history, disliked playing in front of Town fans.

"I must admit I had quite a few chats with Mick about it because it got to the point where it adversely affected me. I preferred playing away.

"A couple of times I thought I've had enough and I'm going to put in a transfer request but Mick was brilliant. He used to have me into his office and said 'why do you worry what they say when it's what I say that really matters?'"

Bizarrely, the closer Town got to promotion in 1980, the more poison was directed Cowling's way.

"It was at home against Halifax at half-time that Mick told me he was taking me off and I couldn't blame him. I was absolutely shattered. The abuse had drained me.

"The *Examiner* ran a piece from Mick saying how disgusted he was at the way the fans treated me.

"He said: 'They can shout as long as they want but I'd still be here long after they stop coming to watch if that's what they want to do.'"

Buxton also leapt to Cowling's defence in his matchday programme notes ahead of the crunch game with Walsall in mid-April.

'Last Saturday, as you all know we beat Halifax 5-0 at home. I should have been over the moon but was far from it," Buxton wrote.

'I was, in fact, very annoyed at the treatment that has been handed out to one of my players. It got to the point where the boy was frightened of making a mistake.

'What annoys me is the fact that this boy will give 150 per cent for this club in every aspect of his trade and has taken criticism through not fault of his own.

"Up to Christmas he could do no wrong and it must be remembered that he has scored ten goals, provided numerous crosses for goals and done sterling work, helping out other players in defensive duties. If every player in the game did that it would surely be a better game.

'If I was a soft manager and we took notice of this unnecessary criticism we would not be in the top four now and if this certain section of supporters want our success to continue they should get used to the name of Dave Cowling on the team-sheet.

"I expect truly loyal supporters to get behind EVERY member of our team because that is what we are, not a collection of individuals, and to give them every help possible."

Buxton also offered staunch support to Cowling privately.

"Anyway, one Friday the old Tannoy had come on – 'Can Dave Cowling come in and see the manager' and everybody looked at me as I was leaving the dressing room.

"I knew what they were all thinking. I feared the worst because it was terrible on a Friday if you got the call to see the manager. It usually meant you weren't playing on the Saturday so I got in there and got straight to the point.

'Fucking hell Mick, what's going off?'

'What you on about?'

'Well I'm obviously not playing tomorrow, am I?'

'Oh aren't you? Well there's the team sheet and you're on it.'

"I thought well that's made me look a twat and he said he just wanted to have a chat with me about a few things to clear the air.

"I continued to get dog's abuse. But I used to think – and excuse me here – 'fuck you, I'll show you' and just get on with it. And in the end I did win the fans over."

Buxton inadvertently helped Cowling by virtue of the biggest mistake of his Town reign – the club-record £110,00-signing of striker Terry Austin in 1980.

"The player who did me the biggest favour ever was Terry because the fans hated him more than they hated me – which was some achievement – so he soaked up the abuse. I used to love it when Mick named Terry on the team-sheet. I'd think 'thank God for that.'

"I travelled in with Terry all the time so I got to know him pretty well. He was a different breed to me and he said he didn't give a shit.

"Terry was very much money-orientated. It was all about what he was getting in his back pocket. He didn't mind about how well he was doing or what people thought.

"I warned Terry about Mick but on the Monday morning, after we'd been beaten on the Saturday, he said he was going in to see the manager. I asked why and he said it was because the gaffer 'was having a go at me and it's knocking my confidence'.

"I didn't think that was a wise move. I tried to get him to think twice: 'Well Terry that's the last thing you do with Mick because you'll be out the door before you know it.'

"But Terry didn't listen and went in for these showdown talks. I was waiting for him because it was his turn to drive us home and he came out.

"I asked: 'How have you got on?' He was ashen-faced. 'He told me I'm leaving. He told me I'd never play for the club again.'"

It did not take long before Austin was offloaded to Doncaster,

"Mick was ruthless. If he thought you were wrong for his team that was it. It didn't matter who you were. If he thought you were upsetting the balance of the side in terms of ethos and effort, he'd show his brutal side.

"That's what happened with Terry. Mick would give him anything but a glowing report. He'd say 'lovely lad but didn't fit in'.

"That episode confirmed to me that Mick had a great knack of getting you to feel really wanted and a great knack of making you feel as though you should leave."

It says a lot about Cowling's strength of character that he shrugged off the vitriol and stuck around to write his name in Town folklore.

But he had already shown steeliness to make his way into the professional game as he grew up on what he describes as the "notorious" Cantley estate in Doncaster.

"I suppose I didn't crumble because of my upbringing which was very much working class.

"My mum, who was a housewife, and dad, who was a postman, were always the sort of people who told us 'if you get knocked down then get back up and have another go.' I had that instilled in me. You just get on with it and prove people wrong.

"You either believe in yourself and think 'right I can do this' or that 'I'm not good enough and it's time to think about doing something else.' I always felt I was good enough.

"Mick Buxton used to say I was just a typically stubborn Yorkshireman. And he's probably right."

Cowling was attracting interest from local clubs while attending Wilby Carr Secondary School and playing for the Doncaster schools team as well as Sunday side Intake Invaders, set up by former England Under-23 international and Doncaster striker Alick Jeffrey.

There was talk about clubs, like Derby when Brian Clough was in charge, being interested in Cowling but his parents intervened. "Mum and dad put their foot down. They wouldn't let me go. They wanted me to complete my education."

Cowling "did okay academically and got decent grades" but sport was his main focus. He was Doncaster's cross-country champion four years on the trot and ruled the 800 and 1,500 metres events for three years as well as playing rugby, cricket and football.

"My parents put such an emphasis on education because they were friends with Alick who kept saying if he's good enough then at 15 or 16 they'll still want to take him on. So don't farm him out to clubs. Let him complete his education and then if something happens, it happens.

"I'm lucky my parents had that attitude. Nowadays, it's common for parents to want it more than kids. Parents are more upset when they get released, which the vast majority do, than their kids are. It's all about reflected glory. I find it quite sad."

Before his football career got moving at Mansfield, Cowling was an apprentice fitter at British Rail where his two brothers worked. "In Doncaster at the time you either went down the pit or went to British Rail."

There was another living to be had by Cowling who impressed enough in a trial match against Mansfield's youth team to sign a YT (youth training) deal and that's where he first came across Buxton, the right-hand man of manager Dave Smith until the latter made way for Peter Morris.

"I'd been called up for England Under-18 trials at the FA's Lilleshall training centre and I came back and everyone was saying it's stitched on you're going to get a contract.

"I went in and the first thing Peter Morris, the bastard, brought me down to earth with a bump.

'Have you got another occupation you can go to?'

'No I haven't – I want to be a footballer'.

'Well we're not prepared to offer you a full-time contract at Mansfield.'

"I was absolutely distraught. My world was falling apart. But then I spoke to a Mansfield youth team coach Jock Basford. He said: 'Don't just walk away. Finish the season and see how things go.'

"I did really well from that point on and Morris called me back in and said I'll give you a contract until the end of the season.

"So I signed on my 17th birthday and at the end of the season he released me again. I'm probably the only player in the world to be released twice by the same club in the same year."

Out of adversity came a new career direction as Cowling put his English O-level to good use.

"I was unfortunate at Mansfield and a lot of people said that to me and I'd had a few offers to go on trial like from Scunthorpe.

"But it was my dad who suggested I send off a few letters to clubs asking for a trial and see what happens.

"I got my head down and wrote how I'd been released by Mansfield and what I'd done like getting an England Under-18 trial and Jock put a covering letter in as well to back me up.

"Fortunately for me, John Haselden, who'd been a physio at Mansfield, read one of them at Huddersfield where he was Tom Johnston's assistant.

"It was only a couple of days later that John, who was from Donnie which must have helped, rang and told me to come up to Huddersfield for a pre-season trial for a week or so because they were looking for left-sided players.

"I went up and he said if nothing happens here I'll sort you out at Sheffield Wednesday. I played in a few games and then Tom Johnston had me in and told me they'd offer me a contract. It was my first professional deal.

"It was painful but getting released and suffering that bitter disappointment was what pushed me forward. You realise that no one in football is going to give you anything on a plate; you're going to have to work for everything you get. So, for want of a better expression, I grafted my balls off.

Rob Stewart's 101 Club journey began at Mick Buxton's Barnsley home.

Town chairman Dean Hoyle fell in love with the Terriers because of Mick Buxton's team.

MP Barry Sheerman discovered what Town meant to Huddersfield people thanks to former Prime Minister Harold Wilson.

Tom Johnston's lasting legacy to Town was bringing Mick Buxton to Leeds Road.

Nellie Thompson was the heartbeat of Huddersfield Town Football Club.

HUDDERSFIELD TOWN

Official
Fixtures
1979 - 80

DIVISION
FOUR

CENTRAL
LEAGUE

The pocket-sized fixture list mapped out the road to glory.

Skipper Peter Hart received a special award after making his 200th Town appearance – at the tender age of 22.

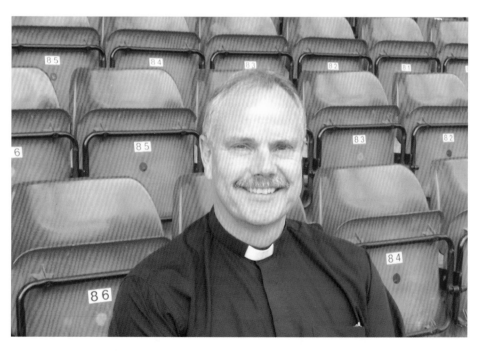

But Town did not require Divine intervention thanks to the work-rate of a player who would swap midfield trenches for the pulpit.

Town fan David Blakeley became the leader of the pack and ended up in the Huddersfield canal.

Midfield maestro Mick Laverick played the role of Town's unsung hero to perfection.

Left: Brian Stanton had an instant impact at Town but he saved his most important deed until after he had hung up his boots by donating a kidney to wife Angela.

Left: Steve Kindon was a larger than life presence on and off the field.

Below: Andy Rankin grabbed the goalkeeper's spot with both hands and didn't let go.

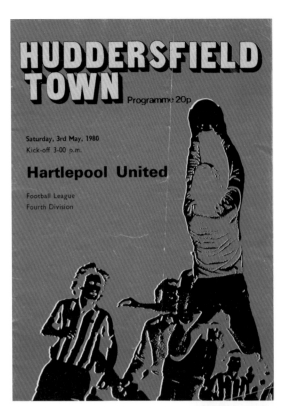

The Town programme was small but almost perfectly formed… …apart from the cigarette adverts

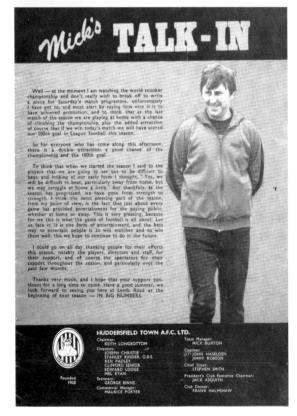

Town's day of destiny was captured by a series of never-seen-before photos taken by fan Chris Telford.

The Champagne was on ice but Town looked down and out against Hartlepool.

Not even the marauding Malcolm Brown could kick-start Town.

Leading goalscorer Ian Robins came to the rescue with a diving header.

Then Robins stooped to conquer to get the promotion party started.

The players led the celebrations with a lap of honour.

Keith Hanvey
provided this photo
which showed he
was generally head
and shoulders
above the
opposition.

Six of the best: Peter Hart, Mick Laverick, Steve Kindon, Fred Robinson, Keith Hanvey and Peter Fletcher show their flare in the civic reception at Huddersfield Town Hall.

The Football League
provided Town with
special mementoes.

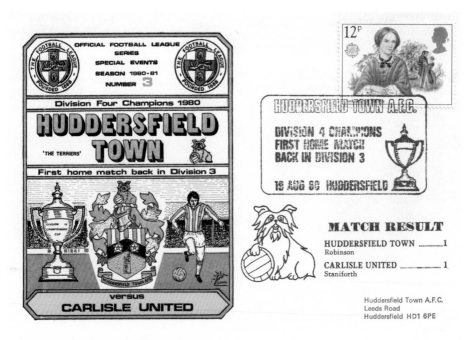

A 'First Day Cover' marked the return of Third Division football to Leeds Road.

Mick Buxton's cherished photo of his stars in blue and white stripes.

Back row (left to right) – Keith Hanvey, Malcolm Brown, Andy Rankin, Dick Taylor, Dave Sutton, Chris Topping; middle row – Mick Buxton (manager), Mick Laverick, Terry Armstrong, Steve Kindon, Peter Fletcher, John Haselden (coach); front row – Dave Cowling, Bernard Purdie, Brian Stanton, Fred Robinson, Ian Robins.

Town fan Tom Bradshaw might not be old enough to remember Mick Buxton's heroes but the former Colne Valley High School student put pen to paper to show them in a different light for The 101 Club.
Top row (left to right): Mick Buxton, Brian Stanton, Peter Fletcher, Andy Rankin.
Second top row: Steve Kindon, Malcolm Brown, Brian Stanton, Ian Robins.
Second bottom row: Peter Hart, Mick Laverick, Dave Sutton, Keith Hanvey.
Bottom row: Mark Lillis, Alan Starling, Fred Robinson, Chris Topping.

"People often think it's plain sailing but it's not. I had a lot of setbacks and disappointments along the way. But it's a case of just grit your teeth and get on with it and I got my reward in the end.

Cowling also had to cope with the new challenge of settling into a new environment at Leeds Road.

"It was hard going into a club that you're unfamiliar with. I'd been at Mansfield where I knew everyone and the pros were great.

"Terry Eccles and Jim McCaffery had already gone from Mansfield to Huddersfield so I did know someone there but I was in with the apprentices so I didn't know anyone. That's another test of character.

"You either think I'll get on with it and if they like me great but if they don't then tough but fortunately for me I got on really well with all the lads.

"Players can be terrible to newcomers. Even I used to look at it this way – I thought I don't want them to do well and I wasn't that bothered if people got injured. It narrowed down the market for the manager."

There was a culture shock in store for Cowling.

"I went into a decent dressing room even though it was absolute chaos. It was run like a holiday camp. Everything seemed to revolve around the snooker table under the main stand.

"Tom would come out and say 'right we're going training, let's get everyone down to the training ground' and half-an-hour later, he'd turn up and half the players were missing. They'd be back at the ground having a snooker tournament.

"You didn't even have proper training kit. It was a shock to me to go into a club like that, from Mansfield, who were relatively successful and so well run. You had to be at the training ground at what ever time the manager decreed. At Huddersfield, the players turned up when they wanted.

"I found it quite sad but there wasn't a great deal of respect for Tom. He'd turn up at the practice ground with a tracksuit on and a shirt and tie and a pair of shoes.

"That meant he wasn't one of those imposing figures where you thought 'Christ, he knows what's he's doing so I'd better be at it.' He'd been a very good manager but at Huddersfield it was quite shambolic.

"He was very old-school. That's not running Tom down. He'd been a very successful manager but that's just how the club was at the time because of the characters in there."

Johnston retired and Buxton's elevation to the manager's office saw Cowling become a first-team fixture following his debut at Barnsley in September 1978.

"The first day Mick became manager I thought something was different. Then I realised he'd got rid of the snooker table but he changed ethics of club completely in a very short space of time.

"His attention to detail was unbelievable. We were probably one of the first teams to watch what we ate. When I first started, players would have steak for pre-match meals and then Mick had us on corn flakes and egg on toast. We even took salt tablets.

"John (Haselden) was a stickler for it. We were playing Lincoln who were up there with us. We got to Lincoln a bit early and they stopped the bus and John took us all for a stroll.

"We were walking along and Ian Holmes popped into a bakery and came out with a big sod-off sausage roll, John saw him and went absolutely ballistic, right in the middle of a busy street.

"It was worth it. We must have been the fittest team in the world that season. We scored more goals then anyone else in the country that season because we just outworked teams."

Cowling became a key player due to his set-piece prowess.

"I was once sat near the front of the team bus and a director leaned over to Mick and asked: 'Why does Cowling take all the corners and free-kicks?'

"Mick just said: 'It's because he knows where he's going to put it and he knows were it needs to be.' That was it for him in a nutshell and I enjoyed the responsibility.

"I remember us being out on Leeds Road playing fields at four o'clock on a Thursday with the whole squad working on set-pieces. If things weren't right, he'd just keep going. At times you'd think

'For fuck's sake, Mick.'

"But he repeated it over and over again and it paid off because something like 50 per cent of our goals came from set-pieces. It was drilled and drilled into us but it paid off handsomely."

Cowling also struck up a good working relationship with left-back Robinson.

"Fred was brilliant for me. I was about nine stone wet-through when I made my debut. I wasn't frightened of tackling but I wouldn't say I was devastating. When Mick moved me wide from a central position, Fred would be like an enforcer for me.

"He used to win the ball and give it to me. It worked fantastically well. I was getting loads of the ball and Fred was doing all the tackling.

"Fred will admit he wasn't the most gifted of players but he was always a great lad to have in your team. I was surprised he didn't go into coaching because he's very knowledgeable and has a lot of good ideas."

Cowling admits he had no idea what was to follow when the 1979-80 season began.

"I thought we could struggle because in pre-season the team hadn't come together after he'd brought in a few players but then we beat Crewe twice in the League Cup and people thought we might be all right.

"We'd been doing well and we were walking back along the canal around Christmas time after training and John just stopped all the squad and gave a little speech: 'You've got to realise now you've got a great chance of going up.'

"That's when people thought right 'let's have no fucking about and let's get it done'. That was the thing about that team. We never laid down, we always worked hard and we did what we were supposed to do."

Cowling, whose personal highlight of the 1979/80 season was a "screamer of a half-volley" in a 1-1 draw with Port Vale, was also able to get revenge on Morris when Town stuffed his Peterborough side 3-0.

"I think I set up all the goals. I know for a fact that Mick Buxton said to him: 'Peter, just explain to me, why did you let Dave Cowling go?' He came out with a line saying he had other senior pros there who were in front of me. Mick said something along the lines of 'well he's come back and haunted you, hasn't he?'"

Cowling had helped Town to the brink of glory but was then left out of the starting line-up for the crunch game with Hartlepool.

"All week Mick had been drumming into us that it would be a hard game but then I was left out because of the abuse I'd been getting after we'd won at Hereford.

"Mick said 'You don't need this' but he put me on at half-time. There was quite a lot of pressure on us and the fans expected us to steamroller Hartlepool but they were a decent side.

"We got there in the end, did a lap of honour and then a lot of it was a bit of a blur but I know we ended up in Johnny's."

....

Dave Cowling played 393 times and scored 48 times for Town but he will always be most fondly remembered for settling one of the most memorable games Leeds Road has ever seen.

That was when Cowling scored the only goal of the match as Town beat Barnsley, featuring a young Mick McCarthy, in a Third Division title tussle in front of 29,801 fans at a jam-packed Leeds Road.

"My kids still take the piss out of me for that goal. They reckon the ball just hit me on the head and dropped in which is just about right.

"I remember the build-up to the goal. Mick Buxton used to get me to make runs across their back four so I could get in behind down the side of the centre-halves.

"I started to make this run and Terry Austin, who hardly put a foot right for us, went in front of me and I was thinking: 'Well, you big stupid bastard get out of the way.' Well he got onto the ball, had a shot that the keeper saved and it spun up and went half way behind me.

"So I just jumped because all I could do was get my head to it and because there was that much spin on the ball, it was thrown forward and just crept into the net. The reaction from the crowd was absolutely deafening."

He had a habit of rising to the occasion and a year later he scored the winner against Newport which sealed promotion to the old Second Division and one that saw Town beat Leeds at Elland Road in the Milk Cup.

"I always get asked about goals against Barnsley, Newport and Leeds. Everyone thought Leeds would spank us but we beat them.

"I never really got nervous before big games because I loved them and for some reason and I always seemed to score in those games."

He left Town in March 1988 and was re-united with Buxton at Scunthorpe where he maintained his knack of scoring momentous goals as he recorded the Iron's first goal at their new £2.5 Glanford Park stadium.

Cowling had played some 600 competitive games when he eventually retired from playing in 1991 before moving into a career in coaching – he holds the coveted Uefa Pro Licence – and having a spell as Doncaster manager before scouting for Fulham and Liverpool.

"Football's been good to me. I'm still busy and I love being involved in the game. I feel very lucky."

Last but not least

Mick Laverick

Mick Laverick had a thing about Ford Capris and the Ford Capri Ghia he owned while he was at Town was his pride and joy.

But it was the fear of coming to the end of the road as a footballer that drove on Laverick rather than the trappings of success like the flashy cars.

"Nowadays footballers, even in League Two are a lot better off than we were and you just have to look in the car parks at clubs like Mansfield to see how well they must get paid," Laverick said over tea and Kit-Kats in the kitchen of his home in the Nottinghamshire village of Ollerton.

"But when people talk about the pressure that footballers are under to deliver because they get paid so much, I have to laugh because I think that it's nothing compared to the pressure we faced as lower league players.

"When you were coming to the end of a contract you knew there'd be nothing left for you in football if you didn't earn yourself a new deal and if you had a young family that was a lot to contend with.

"It was a daunting prospect not having a job when football was all you knew and you had little or no education and mouths to feed.

"You had this uncertainty hanging there. You realised that could be it and your game could be up if you didn't get your contract renewed.

"It was enough to keep you awake at night if things didn't go too well and it certainly kept you on your toes. In actual fact, it spurred me on."

Laverick was the fulcrum of the Town midfield and made 88 appearances and scored 12 goals after he was reunited at Leeds Road with Mick Buxton, who coached him while he was on the books of Mansfield and Southend.

"I was lucky because I sort of followed Mick Buxton around from

Mansfield to Southend to Huddersfield and I was in continuous employment.

"But if you found yourself out of work in those days you'd almost certainly have to move out of football.

"There weren't many of us who went into coaching like Dave Sutton and Dave Cowling because there weren't that many jobs going in football back then.

"There was just a skeleton staff at football clubs compared to how things are nowadays.

"When I was at Town, Mick was the manager and coach, John Haselden was his trainer and physio, Jimmy Robson did the reserves and youth team, and Steve Smith was brought in as chief scout to ease the burden.

"That was it. So jobs behind the scenes were few and far between. It's a far cry from the current state of play where there are loads more jobs going in clubs and also looking out into the community.

"That said I'd never, ever swap what I had in football for what there is now and all the money. I wouldn't have enjoyed playing as much because the game has changed so much."

He had been around the block a few times as a footballer before the Lavericks were able to buy their first family home following to move to Huddersfield and spent £9,750 on a detached place near Mansfield where they would bring up their two sons.

"I might have been a footballer which was a great way to earn a living but we weren't rolling in money.

"The house might not sound like a lot of money but we were stretching ourselves. The mortgage was paid each month but we didn't have much money to throw around and it was never easy to make ends meet but we got by.

"People I knew who were working down the pits in my neck of the woods would have been earning more than me once all their overtime and bonuses were taken into consideration.

"Things change over time and even though I don't like a lot of the play-acting and cheating that goes on in football I don't begrudge the players a penny of what they earn."

They might not have been rich but Laverick and his colleagues were well off in terms of team spirit.

"I suppose it was because we used to go out together for a drink or for a meal in town that we became really good friends and that was reflected in the way we pulled together for each other on the pitch.

"We were just normal people who were on the same money as a lot of the people who'd be in the Junction pub or Johnny's nightclub. We were always an approachable bunch which is probably why people took us to their hearts and why we're still held in high esteem."

Laverick was in the midfield trenches for all but one of Town's 46 Fourth Division matches (he missed one game due to injury) and for some fans he would probably be the last player you would remember from that team.

"The fact Town fans might struggle to remember me doesn't annoy me but it's funny that it sits on my mind. I like to think that people think did a good job and sometimes that's not being selfish and maybe I should have adopted a different way of thinking but that wasn't me.

"Steve Kindon always says that I was Town's unsung hero but I took more than my fair share of stick from the fans.

"He told me I was always one step ahead of the rest of the players and could always see the pass earlier than the rest of the forwards.

"I'd got blamed because sometimes I'd have to hang on to the ball and sometimes got caught or I had to check out and go the other way.

"The first time Steve said that I asked him what he was on about. He said he only realised the truth a long time afterwards. That he could see I was waiting for them to move or make runs or move that never happened."

(For his part, Kindon said: "The fans got on Micky's back but it was my fault. He was lingering on the ball, according to the supporters, but what he was doing was avoiding passing to me because I was offside and while I was coming back onside he'd get tackled.)

Buxton knew enough about Laverick – who was only known as Micky rather than Mick in his Town days - to make a special effort to sign a player that he became acquainted with during his days as a coach when they were together at Mansfield and Southend.

"At Southend we lived five minutes away from each other in Leigh on Sea in club houses so we got to know each other pretty well.

"Before he went to Huddersfield, I'd known he was unhappy with a couple of things but I reassured him the players were still right behind hm.

"But he felt a couple of new players they'd brought in had turned against him and he'd had enough. It's fair to say one or two didn't like his methods but he didn't feel appreciated.

"I didn't want him to go. Mick had made his mind up but I told him that whatever happened I would keep in touch with him."

That is why Buxton made the long trip from Yorkshire to the English Riviera to persuade Laverick to join his Leeds Road revolution.

"Jan and I were down in Torquay for a holiday when I got a call at the hotel and it was Mick. 'Sorry to spoil your holiday but I'll come straight to the point. How do you fancy coming up to Huddersfield?'

"I said 'I don't know Mick' and then he went into his spiel, saying 'I'm going to do this and do that and I've got all these plans and I want you to be part of it. I've spoken to Dave (Smith) and he's willing to let you go. You'll love it up here.'

"I asked him if I could think about but because he'd caught me off guard but he clearly wasn't going to take no for answer: 'I tell you what I'll come down and see you".

Laverick had the credentials to convince Buxton he would be worth the trip to Devon as he had helped Mansfield win the Fourth Division title in 1975 and was in the Southend team that gained promotion to the Third Division in 1979.

"Next thing I know he turned up in the hotel with Maureen and she went off and had a cup of tea with Jan. He didn't have to do too much to talk me into it. The mere fact he was wiling to travel down to Torquay to see me, what a compliment that was, was nearly enough. It would have taken him all day to get there down there.

"I actually ummed and I ahhed at first. It was nice living in Southend. We were settled but my days were numbered, especially if Dave Smith had said I could talk to him. Mick said get out now. You won't regret it. I trusted him.

"He said Town was a big club then it was: 'Get up North - where you belong.' I knew from Mansfield and Southend that he wasn't bullshitting me. I knew morally that he was a good bloke and I believed in what he was saying.

"I had an hour with him, I asked if I could think about it. They stayed for rest of day and that was it. Off he went but only after I agreed to move."

Buxton later explained why he was worth the 600-mile round trip.

"I wanted a midfield player who was technically good and when he'd get a ball it would stick. He fitted the bill perfectly. Good control, good passer, comfortable on the ball. Could see a pass.

"Mick was of our best players. I liked him as a player and a person. He was properly trustworthy. He worked his socks off plus fact he was technically a good player and if he'd been a bit quicker he'd have played at a higher level."

Laverick did attract interest from Tottenham when he was at Southend but had a "stinker" because he knew they were coming to watch him play against York.

In the end, he headed to Leeds Road rather than White Hart Lane, in a player-swap deal that saw fans' favourite Terry Gray go to Roots Hall in June 1979.

"The gaffer told me wanted me to sit in the middle of the park and do what I'd done at Southend which suited me because I always want to be in the thick of it.

"My weak point was that I wasn't the best sprinter but I could go up and down, box-to-box all day. I often think to myself how far could I have gone if I'd had that extra yard or pace, so I could get away from people a little bit quicker.

"A lot of players who really get on are selfish. Ian Robins played up front and was a great goal-scorer. He got all the plaudits because he scored all the goals and he didn't work as hard as his other teammates.

"I tried to please people too much instead of thinking this is about me. I was too much a team player but I loved that and still do.

Maybe that what's Mick saw me. I wasn't interested in whether or not I scored as long we won and I'd done my bit. Maybe I didn't push myself enough."

Laverick was brought up in the pit village of Trimdon in County Durham, but moved to Nottinghamshire where he is now a prison officer, is still clearly a deep thinker when it comes to football.

"What my dad drilled into me sub-consciously when he took me to and from games as a youngster was to be critical of myself and to analyse my own game.

"I know I had my limitations but the one thing I'd never do is hide. That's because of something that really stuck that Mick Buxton had said in a team-talk – and I used it when I was talking to kids I was coaching.

"He told us that it doesn't matter how badly you play, you've got to remember that one, two or three might have a bad game but the week after it might be your turn.

"So if you're having a good game, and things are going well for you, have a look around and give your teammate a bit of a dig because you might need it the week after.

"Everybody can have a bad game but it doesn't matter how badly you play, it doesn't stop you running around. If your touch is off just make sure the bloke you're up against is having as bad a time as you and if things work out for you then you can turn your game round as it goes on.

"In other words, if you're having a stinker, don't put your head up your backside and feel sorry for yourself. If I didn't feel right and up to scratch I'd just think it's going to be one of those days. That was my train of thought.

"I'll accept I'll have a bad game, but I looked at my opponent and thought I'll spoil your day as well. Sometimes you don't think about what you're doing and things improve. Wire into opponent, upset him, not worrying about your own game. See where it takes us."

While Laverick says he feels "privileged that wherever he (Buxton) went he wanted me with him", it opened him up to mockery.

"It's always strange when you arrive at a new club and don't know anyone but I settled in pretty quickly.

"It showed that they'd welcomed me because they always teased me, they gave me light-hearted stick saying that I was Mick's favourite. Keith Hanvey would always joke that I had to sit next to my dad when Mick was around.

"I didn't mind. I found it funny. I had to take it on the chin. But it's fair to say there's no one in football I respect more than Mick because of what he did for me but also because of what he was and is. He stood his ground. He had his beliefs right or wrong. He's a thinker."

According to Laverick, Buxton was "ahead of his time" and there are parallels with the tactics that earned Town a place in the Premier League.

"It's amusing watching the Premier League now with everyone raving about David Wagner and Town and Jurgen Klopp and Liverpool and this high-pressing game. Well, I'm not being funny but we did that when we won the league.

"We used to push up and squeeze the opposition in their own half. Worked hard on closing people down and not letting them play. That was a big principle of ours and it served us well."

Laverick can remember the training sessions designed to get things right on a Saturday as if they were yesterday.

"We'd fine-tune things with a shadow game versus the reserves. Mick would stop the training session when the goalkeeper had possession and told him that as he soon as he rolled the ball out to the full-back a midfielder would close in on him.

"It went from 4-4-2 to 4-2-4 with (Brian) Stanton and (Dave) Cowling falling back in to create a four. The next man would push and if one person didn't do it Mick would blow his whistle give us a lecture.

"He'd go 'what's the point of him sprinting 15 yards to close him down and you're standing six yards off your man and he gets it and turns it's a waste of time so he'd drill the importance of shutting people down into us.

"If you went to stop a cross you had to be no more than a yard away, whoever you are, you spring into the ball and then you slow down, slam the brakes on two or three yards away but then you get down low and stop it and you're not just standing here five yards off him."

Laverick's recollections are testimony to the work ethic that underpinned Town's success under Buxton.

"Players are more athletic now but we were doing that then on heavier pitches when you could tackle and the game was more physical.

"He'd say don't bother going out to crosses if you're not going to go all the way and if you're not going to do it properly then don't do it at all but I won't play you.

"Then he'd show us how it should be done and he'd bend it in like David Beckham used to make his point if we didn't close down properly and it worked.

"No one was allowed to shirk a shift and that's why we're still close as a squad when we meet up because we played as a team all the way through that season.

"There was no back-biting, not even many arguments in training apart from a couple of niggles."

Laverick would leave Town for York in January 1982 after losing his place in the first team to Mark Lillis and after a brief spell back at Leeds Road on loan a year later, he would retire from football in May 1983 after scoring 46 goals in 316 League games

"I was hit by how big the old Leeds Road ground was when I first arrived at Town and how passionate people were about the club.

"It was quite a stage to play your football but we did the place proud. We seemed to steamroller through that season. It was a privilege to be part of something special."

....

Mick Laverick thought the world of Mick Buxton but it was another former Town manager in the shape of Bill Shankly who looms largest in his football memories.

Laverick and his Southend teammates were getting ready for an FA Cup replay at Anfield in January 1979 against reigning European

champions Liverpool when former Reds boss Shankly delivered the team talk of their lives.

"We'd had a practice session at Everton's Bellefield training ground and when we got back to the dressing room.

"Dave Smith, our manager, said, 'there's someone I want you all to meet, a friend of mine who'll talk to you about playing Liverpool, so grab yourselves a cup of tea and sit down'.

"There was a little knock on the door and in walks Bill Shankly and all the lads were looking at each other, wondering: 'Are we seeing things?' He had the lads eating out of his hand. We were sat there open-mouthed."

'You'll never have experienced anything like Anfield but don't let it intimate you.'

'Don't forget when you go down that tunnel to touch that famous 'This is Anfield' sign.

'That will get you in the right frame of mind because you'll be going into a cauldron of noise.'

"I hung on his every word. I couldn't wait to get out there and I didn't care what happened at the end of it."

Laverick was raring to go but nothing could prepare him for the moment the teams emerged from the tunnel before a 37,797-strong gallery.

"I looked around and thought 'Christ almighty there's nothing like it.' It was like an electric shock going through me but I raised my game and did pretty well..

"There were a couple of times when I did things and I know this sounds cheesy but I was marking Graeme Souness and he tapped me on the head and said: 'Good bit of skill that son well done.'

"When we finished there was no swapping shirts. They didn't give them away in those days. But what more than made up for that is that all their players ushered us down towards the famous Kop.

"Thanks to them I'll never forget that walk facing the Kop and seeing a mass of hands clapping. That's why I'll always have a soft for Liverpool."

False teeth, Mars bars and cigarettes

by Mark Lillis

It might seem odd because I couldn't get in the Town team at all throughout that legendary 1979/80 season but I learned so much from all the players.

I'd got into the first team and played a handful of games the previous season and even though I was on the fringes of the squad I felt I came on leaps and bounds because they were inspirational.

It was almost a brotherly thing. I was working with good people who were happy to share their vast experience with younger players like me who were trying to make their mark in the game because of a tremendous togetherness.

They watched your back and it you weren't doing something right they'd take you to one side and have a word.

You only had one sub in those days so I didn't even get a look-in but I stood in the tunnel before every game and patted every one of them on the back and wished them well.

If things didn't go well in matches the players sorted things out at half-time. If someone wasn't pulling their weight, they got told.

I waited in the tunnel when we won the title and I gave them all a big hug. I did that because they were my teammates and I was proud of them.

It was a fantastic achievement and I wanted to be part of the team but it felt that we were all together.

They raised the bar that season and when I eventually got into the team I knew I had to be at the top of my game.

I especially owed a lot to Steve Kindon who was one of the head boys of the dressing room.

I got fitter because I had to give him piggyback lifts up Kilner Bank in pre-season training and he was quite a size but he also made me feel welcome.

Every Monday it would be a case of Steve asking 'where did you do Saturday night, then?'

'Just went into Manchester, went to a nightclub and then went for a curry – bhunna chicken, half-rice, half chips.

'Is that all you eat?'

He nicknamed me 'bhunna' and it's stuck.

Mick Buxton knew exactly who needed an arm around them like Brian Stanton and Ian Robins and who needed a kick up the backside like me.

He once told my dad he sometimes thought I'd stick one on his chin after one dressing down. He said I was like a little leaf floating in the wind.

Apparently, I turned into the Incredible Hulk because he'd wound me up so much. I puffed my chest out, pulled back my shoulders and walked out raring to go.

There will always be an especially big place in my heart for Andy Rankin, who used to pick me up from my girlfriend's house on the way to training.

Andy would tip me off about a few things in life and share a few words of wisdom on football on the way in.

Then you'd go into the dressing room and he'd take his false teeth out, have his Mars bar and then have a fag. You wouldn't get away with that now.

View from the Cowshed

by Town fan Andy Shuter

Growing up in a tough Northern town like Heckmondwike in the late 70s/early 80s wouldn't be everyone's ideal choice if they had it.

For those who don't know it, 'Hecky' is located pretty much equidistant between Leeds and Huddersfield on the A62.

It's a very working class place with three big council estates and you either go there to visit family, you're lost or the M62 is closed at Gildersome.

The year is 1979 and, as I was from a Catholic family, I was nearing the end of my primary school education at Holy Spirit school on Bath Road.

The nearest Catholic secondary school was St John Fisher in Dewsbury, which although was a few miles away, filled me with quite a bit of relief as it meant I escaped the perilous trip to White Lee, locally referred to as 'The Headbangers' School'. Incidentally, Deano (Dean Hoyle) went there, but don't tell him I told you so.

Margaret Thatcher had just come to power and was on a mission to crush the unions and the working class in general. My dad, a staunch union railwayman hated her. The North-South divide was only going one way and generally the outlook in these and other areas was, well pretty grim.

My dad (God rest his soul) was football-nuts and had seen pretty much all of the greats play. By birth, he was a Blackpool fan and regularly used to tell me about the famous 1953 FA Cup-winning side (I can name that side to this day).

Throughout his formative years, he regularly watched great sides such as Preston North End, Bolton Wanderers, Man United, Liverpool, Everton and Burnley who all had iconic players. I need not mention any names, you know who they are and they are etched in football folklore forever.

But the one thing that he always used to say was this: 'Son, when it's YOUR team that achieves something, it means everything.' Of course he was referring to the famous 'Matthews final' of 1953.

During the mid 1970s, my dad had taken me to many grounds watching many different clubs (including L**ds) but I never really felt at home. It wasn't until around 1978 when I asked him to take me to watch Huddersfield Town that things changed forever.

"Huddersfield Town???" he shrieked. "Why on earth would you want to go and watch that rubbish?" (I've often asked myself the very same question!).

But true to his love of the game, and my persistence, he took me to a Fourth Division "clash" against Torquay on a wet Tuesday night in front of about 3,500 hardy souls.

I can't remember much more about that night (other than going on the bus and the stinky bogs) but even though we only drew and were near the bottom of the Football League, something just felt right.

Don't ask me to explain what that means because I still don't know, but those who know, just know.

Not long after, my dad came home from work with his usual copy of the Daily Mirror and told me that some bloke called "Mick Buxton" had taken over as manager and that he had read all about how he was going to make Huddersfield Town great again.

He chuckled to himself and made some quip about "platting fog" or something like that, as I'm sure many others also did.

Not surprisingly, many of the kids at school followed the "glory" sides such as Man U, Liverpool and of course our friends from down the A62, but I noticed that there were a few Town fans in our ranks. Not that many, but still a few.

Whilst playing football at the local rec, some lads came up to me and asked who I supported. This, sadly, was a common trick to give you a good beating if you didn't give the right answer.

But I knew that 'Hopper' (a small ginger kid from Hecky (whose mum was a dinner lady at our school) was indeed a Town fan, so I of course told them I was Huddersfield too. I was now in the club.

"Half-one 221 bus from Hecky on Saturday, Shuter. We've got Port Vale at home, you can come with us, dun't be late."

But of course I was only 10 years old at this time and these were older boys, so I couldn't possibly expect my mum and dad to let me go.

After considering and discounting all the devious options (and of course my mum's slipper), I decided to tell my dad and ask him if I could go on my own. NOT A CHANCE!

But he did agree to take me, which was a fair compromise. So there we are, the date is 22nd of September 1979, my first "proper" Town game.

My dad, who was far more switched on than I ever gave him credit for, knew the score. Town had started the season brightly and had won all but three of their first few games and were sitting fourth.

It was Saturday lunchtime and the pubs in 'Hecky' were packed with Town fans of all ages.

Kids weren't allowed in to pubs then, so whilst your dad was enjoying a pint inside a smoky taproom (like I said, he knew the score!), you were given pop 'n' crisps and left outside with the other kids.

Of course, someone inevitably had a football and before too long a couple of jumpers went down for goalposts, and the New Inn car park was transformed into 'Leeds Road'.

This is the first time I ever heard the names Robins, Laverick, Hart and Fletcher as the kids belted the ball towards the 'goals'.

I'm sure they will be star-struck when they read this! Hopper and his mates were, of course, there and had no problems with that fact that "Tommy" was there too, as were many other dads, and indeed granddads. A true family feeling.

Pretty much everything after that is a blur. But of course how could I forget that we won that game 7-1. I also remember some bloke with a foreign sounding name (Bob Delgado) scoring an own goal (the crowd were taunting him).

But the most vivid memory though were those majestic blue and white stripes (the team I saw a year of so prior to this wore a plain navy shirt). They were regal, traditional and just bloody majestic. No more needs to be said really.

The rest is history as they say and the rest of that season will be more than covered in better detail than I could ever describe.

As I write this, Town have just gained promotion to the hallowed Premier League and are preparing for their first home game versus Newcastle.

As I look to the sky and toast my old man, I can truly now understand what he meant about Blackpool winning the cup in 1953. When it's YOUR team, it means so much more. UTT WAPL!!!

Sheets to the wind

by Martin Sykes

However good it was, and Johnny's Night Club will hold a special place in the hearts of Huddersfield people of a certain age who experienced their 1970s/1980s heyday, it could sometimes be a little dull through repetition.

This led to such larrikins as setting off fire extinguishers, trying to buy them out of matches, "escaping" over the fence in the open bit, playing Jesus and Mary Chain's "April Skies" over and over to annoy and delight in equal measure and other harmless japes (unless there was, you know, an actual fire).

But on one Friday night in early May 1980, talk was dominated by Huddersfield Town.

For context, the people involved had seen their football club floundering in hell for much of the previous decade after starting it in spectacular style. Now, Town stood on the verge of redemption and were to escape the bottom division at long last – it is hard to overstate just how dismal the preceding years were.

Buxton's side of rejects, misfits and journeymen had rekindled interest, excited the supporters and were writing themselves in to HTFC folklore yet, and yet, all of their efforts were in danger of being diluted by not being crowned Division 4 champions and confirming their deserved status as the best in the division. An Alan Buckley inspired Walsall threatened the coronation and victory over Hartlepool United in the last game was needed.

The occasion, it was agreed in the Jungle Bar, demanded a gesture and a banner was decided upon. In these days of the NSL and their wonderfully creative efforts, it is easy to forget that this expression of support was rare and amateurish.

Fuelled by a typical pre nightclub town centre pub crawl – Shoehorn, Painted Wagon, Plumbers Arms, West Riding et al – talk turned to a slogan. Alternative ideas were scorned and spurned before consensus was reached with "Ian Robins lays on more balls than Fiona Richmond". The identity of the author has been lost in the mists of time (it was me, actually), but it was seized upon despite its lack of brevity, and mostly because of Fiona.

The easy availability of porn, overt sexuality of celebrities (some of whom are celebrated solely because of it) and all pervasive sexual imagery would render Fiona pretty redundant, or, at best, run of the mill, these days but in the late 70s she built herself a fortune through the medium of sex.

A vicar's daughter (thank you Wikipedia), she defied convention and portrayed herself as a woman who didn't give a hoot that people would attack her relentlessly for her choices but, more importantly in the context of our banner, she was football related because of an escapade involving that arch self publicist Malcolm Allison and the Crystal Palace players' bath.

Ian Robins, meanwhile, was not only the club's leading scorer in that memorable season, his partnerships with, first, Peter Fletcher and then Steve Kindon were symbiotic. Between the 3 of them, they scored 56 goals with Ian bagging 25. Assists were not routinely recorded back then as they are now, but it isn't difficult to imagine Robins' contribution to the tallies of his strike partners and others.

Having chosen the words for the placard, the rather more difficult feat of actually creating it was discussed. Drunken agreement of a time and place - fairly early morning at the offices of one of the participants with access to materials - was achieved but likely attendance still dubious.

Perhaps the fervour excited by that Buxton team was too visceral to miss; enough hands appeared and work began with extra strong paper and black paint.

One or two had a pretty decent design background allowing the space to be filled with some precision and no words were left off or scrunched in to space - it was a damned good effort in which I took no part whatsoever.

The paper was then nailed to strategically aligned four by twos and the banner, in all its glory, was complete.

Practical considerations, which perhaps should have been thought about before embarkation, started to kick in and mainly concerned how to get the bloody thing in to the ground. Which part of the ground should have been a simpler question, but that particular Saturday was blighted by quite strong winds - the banner was aesthetically pleasing but hardly engineered to stringent standards.

Out came the nails as it became obvious that the component parts would have to be smuggled in to Leeds Road - the large pieces of wood could, conceivably, be perceived as weapons even if the visitors' support would be minuscule at best - and reassembly would have to take place in the ground.

Then came location. Obviously, the main stand was out and the Cowshed was going to be rammed, but the East terrace and the open end were both viable. The terrace offered shelter from the wind but, with the roof, less visibility so it was decided that despite its exposure to the elements, the Bradley Mills end would host the spectacle.

With less than military precision, the wooden poles were stuck down trouser legs, the banner furled under a jacket and stiff legged approaches made to the turnstiles. Remarkably, the odd policeman encountered was more Clouseau than Poirot and the parts were in the arena.

With assembly already practised, all be it uninterrupted by wind or authorities, the banner was ready quite quickly and laid out on the concrete steps at the back of the open end.

As the match started in front of nearly 17,000, the call was made for the big reveal. The choreography proved flawless and up it went to appreciative noises, lasting a few minutes before the "extra strong" paper easily lost the battle with the now raging nor'easter.

We felt we had done our bit, the *Examiner* got a (unpublished but archived) photo, and Town secured a 2-1 victory (after going in at half time one down).

Naturally, Ian Robins scored both goals. Walsall lost and the League title was secured.

Fiona is now a hotelier.

Insurance cover

Bernard Purdie

They say you can't believe everything you read in newspapers and Bernard Purdie is living proof that old adage could very well be true.

Just before he moved to Huddersfield, it was in good faith that his local paper had reported that Purdie had upped sticks and left Crewe Alexandra for Stockport County.

Purdie had indeed held talks with Stockport player-manager Mike Summerbee about a transfer to Edgeley Park but reports of his Crewe demise had been greatly exaggerated

He had decided against a move but Crewe manager Tony Waddington was so certain his long-serving captain was quitting Gresty Road that he had jumped the gun and mistakenly briefed journalists that he'd gone.

"It was a funny old business," the 68-year-old Purdie said from his home in Wrexham, North Wales.

"Tony Waddington was my boss and he said 'you're going to Stockport' so I arranged to go and meet Mike Summerbee for a chat and got on a train to go meet him.

"I went with an open mind but it turned out that move just wasn't for me. As a player, Summerbee was a Manchester City legend but didn't impress me as a manager.

"The things he was saying didn't connect with me so I went back to Crewe, went to see the manager and we had a conversation along the lines of:

'Sorry, but I'm not going.'

'But you've got to go – I've already spent the money.'

'Sorry. It just wasn't there. It didn't seem right.'

"I stuck to my guns. The trouble was, it was all over the local press, in black and white, that I had signed for Stockport and that was because of Tony Waddington.

"This was on a Thursday but I was captain of Crewe at the time and I still ended up leading the team out on the Saturday.

"It was all a bit embarrassing for the club. People were turning round saying: 'What the bloody hell is going on? You're not supposed to be here.'"

Word got round and Town boss Mick Buxton wasted no time in getting in touch with Waddington for a versatile player who had gone from Wrexham to Chester to Crewe.

"On the Monday I got a phone call from Micky Buxton and the difference between him and Mike Summerbee was massive.

"I believed in what Buxton was building at Huddersfield and what he wanted from me. I had no hesitation in saying I would move. He impressed me with the way he spoke.

"He was passionate; Summerbee was just the opposite. His heart didn't seem in it. I got the feeling Buxton wanted me and when you get that feeling it makes one hell of a difference."

Buxton had set his sights on Purdie after Town had played and beaten Crewe three times early on in that 1979/80 season – twice in the League Cup and once in the Fourth Division.

"I played centre forward in one game, central midfield in the other and centre-half in the other one.

"He said I was his insurance policy on promotion: 'You can play anywhere and if I have a problem I can slot you in.'

"He wanted me as cover in all departments and was true to his word. I ended up as full-back when we won the Fourth Division but I played in every position bar goalkeeper when I was at Town."

Purdie came in at left-back when Fred Robinson was injured and retained his place until the end of the season.

"Buxton told me when everyone was fit I wouldn't get in the team.

"That's how honest he was when we first talked and he repeated that same thing again after I'd signed.

"I'd be on the bench when everyone was available. But it didn't put me off. I wanted the challenge.

"My attitude was: 'We'll see how we go and if I get in the team, I'll have to make sure you have to keep me there.'"

Purdie had moved for £22,000 and ended up being paid £180 a week, "which was excellent because in the lower divisions if you were successful you'd get well paid because of the bonus system."

Town gave Purdie a chance to move up in the world but his upward mobility was eclipsed by goalkeeper Bruce Grobbelaar who played his first Football League matches at Crewe before reaching the summit of European football with Liverpool.

"I wanted that move to see if I could move up a gear and Huddersfield gave me the chance to test myself at a higher level because I'd never played in a good side.

"I'd played for Crewe for nine years and at times I was linked with moves away but they never happened. I was going to Watford when Mick Buxton was there as coach and Crystal Palace and you end up thinking a move up would never materialise.

"I'd always been in a struggling side where you went out just trying to keep the score down. At Crewe, I'd not been used to winning too often but then all of a sudden that all changed.

"There was a winning mentality at Town which was down to Micky Buxton's work ethic and his staff. We worked our socks off and no one did that better than Steve Kindon up front who was our star player. We made him run all over the place."

One of seven children, Purdie was brought up in a mining community in the village of Brynteg in the Wrexham area. His dad worked as a miner in the Gresford colliery, a place where 266 men had perished in a massive underground explosion in September 1934.

"I came from a very poor background. We didn't have much money but we were happy.

"There were no computers in those days so you went out and messed around, climbed trees or played football to keep yourself entertained.

"I got into playing football which was the only activity we did because it didn't cost anything, apart from the price of the pair of boots you got for Christmas.

"I couldn't play enough football. I don't want to sound big-headed or anything like that but I was head-and-shoulders above the people around me.

"But my dad always used to say it's one thing being the best in your village but you've got to be the best in the larger Wrexham area and beyond. Who knows what's out there for you?'

"And so I did go further afield and I went everywhere by bus. There was no ferrying kids around by parents like there is now. There weren't any cars about in those days."

Despite his footballing prowess, a life in mining beckoned and he spent six months training and then six months down the pit as an apprentice electrician.

"When you left school at 16 you'd follow your dad down the coalmine and so a couple of my brothers and I went down the pit but it didn't last long for me.

"A friend of mine broke both his legs in an accident. It was awful. He was hit by a runaway wagon when he was taking stuff to the coalface.

"It had come off the rails and pinned him up against a wall. That's when I thought mining was not for me. Good night, God bless. I left the pit two weeks later."

He went to work at Shotton steelworks and yet played football for the rival Brymbo plant, which had a highly-regarded works team and that's where he was spotted by Wrexham scouts at the age of 17.

"My first ambition was to play football, my second ambition was to play for Wrexham and my third ambition was to play for Wales and I had done all three by age of 17.

"But achieving all your ambitions before you're 18 isn't always a good idea. You tend to think I've done it and things peter out but thankfully it didn't do me any harm.

"I spent 19 years as a professional and the three years I had at Huddersfield were the best footballing years of my life. And I'm not just saying that.

"I've got shirts and caps from the times I played for the Wales youth team but as a professional my pride and joy is my Fourth Division championship medal that I won at Huddersfield."

Purdie and his first wife and their three children moved to the Waterloo area of Huddersfield area and bought a three-storey house in Round Wood Avenue where average house prices are now £125,000.

"The people were absolutely brilliant with us which might have been because we were successful.

"We brought good times to Huddersfield and we put smiles on people's faces around the town after some lean years. I made great friends and still send them Christmas cards.

"I got my head down and fitted into the squad and the football went well, especially at left-back, because of Dave Cowling working up and down the wing.

"He worked the flank so hard I rarely got taken on by speed merchants because he was always in front of me.

"He wasn't the fans' favourite but he worked his socks off in just the way as Brian Stanton did on the other flank and he could do no wrong in the fans' eyes."

Purdie's parents, Jack and Lily, also relished his new lease of life and regularly headed over the Pennines to watch their son in action.

"Huddersfield Town was a First Division club that had slipped up but they retained a lot of the old habits which died hard and there were always two men in uniforms at the door to welcome you on match days.

"It was a real novelty, especially for my Mum who had never seen me play before I went to Huddersfield but they had seats that took her into the directors' box and their suite at half-time and full-time and she was absolutely taken aback.

"She had to pinch herself because here was this mother-of-seven whose husband was a miner, rubbing shoulders with the great and the good of Huddersfield in these ever-so-plush surroundings with great food laid out on the table for all the guests.

"They kept these little things going and my mum loved everything about those traditions. Afterwards, she had nothing to say about the games but she couldn't stop talking about the hospitality which she thought was absolutely wonderful."

....

After leaving Town, Purdie returned to his Wrexham roots and played for Crewe before having a spell at Bangor in Northern Premier League but quit when "my legs started to go".

Lots of manufacturing jobs were available on the local industrial estates but he "didn't fancy that for 10 hours at a time" and ended up spending 26 years "walking round the town and becoming well known" as a postman until retirement at the age of 60.

The young-at-heart Purdie has been married to his second wife, Joanne, for 22 years, and together they have two teenage children, Alex, who is studying at university in Liverpool, and 14-year-old Bethan.

"Bethan really keeps me on my toes. She is a Welsh international gymnast and I ferry here all over the country. 'Dad can you take me here?' and 'Dad can you take me there?' It's a labour of love."

The old ones are the best

Andy Rankin

Andy Rankin and his family were making painfully slow progress on their journey up the M1 on their way to Huddersfield.

The goalkeeper had to keep pulling the family car into the service stations dotted alongside the motorway because his wife, Margaret, was so upset at the family being uprooted.

They were heading from Watford to Huddersfield and while it is move that worked out well for Rankin on the field, the mixed emotions among his family are a reminder that the nomadic lifestyle of a footballer can be tough on loved ones.

"My sole purpose was to play for as long as I could but it was a big upheaval for us as a family," Rankin said in his Holme Valley home.

"Recently, I was speaking to my daughter, Emma, who is living in Canada, and now I realise more than ever that they were actually glad to leave Watford.

"I felt our children were being uprooted and so it would be hard on them but when you're playing football your kids get stick at school and it's a bit hard for them, to say the least.

"But my wife, Margaret, was really distraught that we were leaving, so much so that we had to stop at every service station on the M1. We were leaving a lovely home and lots of friends in the area so I could understand why she was upset.

"It was a big one but we had to do it because in football, the manager has to run the club as he sees fit and if you are part of the fall-out that's just how it is.

"Watford even sent one lad round to our home, which was a club house, to look at it when we were still in it. He knocked on the door, he was sorry but he was just doing what he'd been told to do. There was no messing about. It was pretty heartless but it can be a ruthless business."

It seems apt that former Rankin lives right in the heart of Last of the Summer Wine country.

As he looks back, over a cup of tea, on a football career that spanned 20 years, you can't help but feel he would be in good company with Compo, Foggy and Clegg.

The madcap trio may no longer be roaming the Holme Valley and Compo has stopped pestering Nora Batty but 73-year-old Rankin continues to show the old ones are still the best.

He was 35-years-old – just a year younger than manager Mick Buxton - when he was brought from Watford to Huddersfield when Richard Taylor and then Alan Starling were sidelined by injury.

Liverpool-born Rankin headed to West Yorkshire thinking it would be a temporary stay but ended up liking the place so much he has been here ever since and now calls Thongsbridge home.

Rankin had been around the block quite a few times when he joined Town and that experience taught him that he was on to a good thing at a club fighting its way out of the Fourth Division.

"You could call them misfits and cast-offs and this, that and the other but after about ten minutes of my debut I thought: 'Bloody hell this is one good team.'

"They were very fit, they had little patterns from set-pieces and the whole thing was so professional it wasn't anything like a rag-tag and bobtail team.

"They were excellent. They were too good for the Fourth Division. I was chuffed when I saw them in action. I thought this will be enjoyable and it turned out to be blinking marvellous."

Rankin made his debut in a 5-1 win over Rochdale at Leeds Road just before Christmas and performed so well that a month later he was offered a long-term deal and did not miss another game that season.

"I was just asked to come and play a few games and I was expecting to return to Watford but Mick Buxton kept me in.

"I thought this 'will do for me' as long as I was playing all right and they didn't end up telling me to bugger off."

After beginning his career at Everton, the Scouser had played 299 times for Watford ("I was told I wouldn't play 300. I'll just say that.") when he became surplus to requirements when Graham Taylor was manager.

"We were training at Honeypot Lane and I suddenly saw Graham run across the field, speeding towards me and I thought 'hang on a minute'.

"He goes, 'Mick Buxton's on the phone, I think it's a move, you'd better get up there straight away' which shows how keen he was for me to leave."

Rankin "jumped at the chance" of joining Buxton who knew he would be a safe pair of hands having worked with him closely as a coach and physio at Vicarage Road.

"Mick was a good motivator and very good man-manager and he was a deep thinker. He once told me he was reading PG Wodehouse. I was thinking 'fair enough, I just want to get my boots on and get out there'.

"Mick had the German thinking on the game with his high-pressing tactics. The pieces just fitted together perfectly with Malcolm Brown overlapping Brian Stanton down the right and Dave Cowling and Fred Robinson combining down the left."

Rankin brought a wealth of experience to Town that proved crucial in the closing stages of the title race.

He had been on Everton's books as a schoolboy and would make a 15-mile journey on his Carlton racing bike to practice sessions at the club's Bellefield training complex.

He landed a white-collar, office job for a company called Mersey Cables while he honed his football skills with Everton but then got the thumbs-down before grabbing a second opportunity with both hands.

"They told me they didn't think I was going to make it. They just said I wasn't tough enough or didn't have this, that and the other. They never fully explained, they just said 'that's it'.

"So I ended up joining the police cadets but one day the sergeant called me through to his office and said Everton had been in touch and wanted me for their youth team at Old Trafford.

"I went along and got on the team bus but it was clear the players weren't too fond of me because their mate was injured and they didn't want me nicking his place but the long and short of it was that I had a great game and I went full-time."

A 2-2 draw in his senior debut against Nottingham Forest was followed by a Fairs Cup tie against Rangers at Ibrox when "all you could smell in the goalmouth was the reek of booze".

There was also a game against Stoke when he broke his hand, had it bandaged up and played the rest of the game on the wing and "almost scored".

He also has a tale to tell about his Merseyside derby against Liverpool, which shows how little protection goalkeepers received from referees.

"John Toshack had gone behind me and as I jumped for a cross he just pulled my arm down. The ball dropped down and, bang, it was in the net. He did it well. The referee saw nothing untoward. I was the villain. That's the way it goes. I don't do self-pitying."

It was after a club trip to Israel that he learned from teammates that his days were numbered before being told of Watford's interest.

"I wasn't bothered. I just wanted to play so I went home and told Margaret we're going to Watford. She said where's that? I told here I thought it was up in the North East. That's the God's honest truth."

Rankin was on £30-a-week at Everton but as a parting gift he was granted a £20 rise by manager Harry Catterick to ensure he got a decent deal and Watford paid him another tenner.

But for Rankin nothing encapsulates better what it was like to be a footballer than the second-hand car that Everton striker Joe Royle sold him before he left Goodison Park.

"That thing kept me really fit. It was so temperamental you never knew if it would start or not.

"One day it was pouring down and the bloody thing wouldn't start. I had to ask Margaret to get in the car, drop the clutch in, I'd push and soon as it fires up, she was to lift the clutch and put it in neutral.

"Off we went down the road, the car fires up, she suddenly bursts forward and I fell flat on my face. I thought she was going to put it in reverse, come back and take her chances but luckily she resisted the temptation, probably because she was laughing so much."

Rankin is not too good on the specifics of the 1979/80 season but he was booked for the only time in his distinguished career when a penalty was awarded in a 1-1 draw at Hartlepool but more importantly he kept eight clean sheets in 24 appearances.

This included an *Examiner* man-of-the-match performance on his return to Merseyside when Town drew 0-0 at Tranmere when reporter Paul Clark was fulsome in his praise for a series of full-length and reflex saves.

Rankin continued to serve Town with distinction until he had a brush with death.

"We were playing Shrewsbury in the FA Cup. Three or four of us went for the ball at the near post, I dived out, a player dived in and I got a bang on the back of the head.

"Next thing I know is that I'm laying in a hospital bed, covered in mud with my gear on, wondering what's happened. Steve Kindon came in with a beer and the staff went mad with him but I thought he was doing the right thing.

"I had a pee and couldn't think what had happened. It was a fractured skull and I'd gone to St Luke's Hospital in Huddersfield. I had an x-ray and I thought they were going to say there was nothing in there at first.

"The doctors asked me if had any other means of earning a living but the physio (John Haselden) promised me that he'd get me back playing. I started playing again but my goal kicks were even worse than they were before.

"Things were bit foggy but at one point someone rang us up when we were living in Shelley with a view to buying the house and I agreed a price but it was way out.

"My wife saw what was happening, thought 'wow' and quashed it straight away. Thankfully there have been no repercussions since."

The head injury spelled the beginning of the end of Rankin's career and Buxton feared the worst when he started being able to beat his goalkeeper during practice sessions.

"We were playing Man City and got hammered. I thought this was awful. I didn't feel as though I was letting them down but we were being ripped to bits.

"But still, afterwards, the defeat was put down to me. I wasn't one to have a go back I just said 'okay, okay, if that's how you see it, fair enough' but it just dwindled from then on.

"And then they said they weren't renewing my contract. Mick sat me down. I don't think you're getting there like you used to. I don't think you're doing it. I couldn't complain.

"It would have been a lot better if I'd have had my head right but there we go. That's life but I still feel very fortunate as I played till I was 38."

The Rankins and their four children had been living in Shelley area of Huddersfield but suddenly everything fell apart after his Town days abruptly ended.

"It had been the first chance we'd had to get a mortgage so we started after my move to Huddersfield and got a house in Shelley and it was nice up there.

"I'd had a little arrangement with the club. It was written into my contract. They renewed it, we worked off that, that the money was there to pay the mortgage.

"And then the bank got in touch with us. I said the money was there and they said no it's not. I remember coming home and saying to Margaret, 'I think we're in the shit here,'

"The contract was in the unit in the kitchen. I took it out to have a look and there it was: contract provisions - nothing.

"I hadn't looked at it. I had just gone on a previous arrangement. There wasn't a financial advisor or agent in sight in those days. I wish there had been.

"I finished in 1982 and within a month or two we were out of the house and down here in Thongsbridge.

"I was in a state of shock more than anything else. It was a lovely house but you've got to carry on. Margaret was sat in the front room crying; I thought 'bloody hell'. I should have looked at my contract."

After football, he found work Tarmacing roads and then took on a job at his local hospital driving its mobile clinic before, for 18 years, becoming a forklift truck in the warehouse at a printers in Denby Dale.

"It was a big change after being outdoors all day earning a living, doing nights, doing shifts that changed all over the place. But it brought us money in to live, thank God."

Despite the fractured skull and a severe case of concussion which left him hospitalised after a Watford match at Bristol Rovers, when Buxton was his coach, he remains in rude health with the exception of a bit of tinnitus.

That is even though he has smoked since the age of 17 apart from a ten-month spell when he quit after surgery in Leeds to tackle angina in 1999.

"A couple of us would light up in the dressing room at Huddersfield. It's amazing how much it's changed – it even cost that lad at Arsenal £20,000 when he sparked up after having a bit of a wobbly one.

"I hope I don't sound morbid but I'm just grateful to be about. I'd like to think I'm healthy. I'm not as in good a shape as I was a couple of years ago because as you get older, it seems to accelerate.

"But the good thing is that we haven't got to do anything but enjoy our retirement, pottering around the house or me scootering around on my motorbike."

He does not attend re-unions or go to Town matches because he is "a firm believer that once you come away, you come away" but he has countless memories.

"What I do realise that I've experienced the sort of highs that most football fans would give their right arm for. Now I couldn't imagine stepping on to a football pitch but it just used to seem like the most natural thing in the world.

"One thing I found a bit odd is that someone once said to my son 'your old man liked showing his arse.' I always wondered where this came from. Now I know it was a case of mistaken identity."

....

Andy Rankin's move to Huddersfield proved to be one of those things that are worth waiting for.

It was in March 1968 that the Liverpool Echo newspaper reported that Rankin had signed for Town in a £25,000 deal and was all set to make his debut against Derby.

However, a few days later it transpired that the deal had broken down due to a medical problem.

"It's true that I was supposed to come to Huddersfield in 1968. Our manager, Harry Catterick, told me they wanted me and I thought great because I was hungry to play.

"So I went home, got changed, went across the Pennines and met Town manager Ian Greaves who sent me for a medical.

"I went back to Everton and Harry sat me down said he doesn't want you anymore. I'd been out the wrong night.

"I told Harry I'd been out and he said 'I know, everyone's been out but you chose to go out on the wrong night."

The Unsung Heroes

by Mick Buxton

Mick Buxton may have used just 16 players as Town clinched the Fourth Division title but he insists that several more people behind the scenes also played crucial rules but are unknown to most fans.

Buxton was supported by his own small but perfectly formed backroom team and he is keen to point out there were other club employees who were never in the limelight but were vitally important parts of the fabric of the club.

Right from Nellie Thompson, who washed the kit, to Fred Elms who almost gave his right hand for the club, they will go down as legends by almost every Town player who came across them at Leeds Road.

"The coaching staff and me didn't have set meetings to discuss things but we were always discussing what was going on at the club and how individual players were getting on," Buxton said.

"There were only a few of us doing everything on a shoestring but we worked well together and I always listened to their advice but I always took the final decisions and what I said would go."

Here Buxton, looks back at the contribution of the club's unsung heroes.

First team coach and physiotherapist John Haselden

John was very firm with people and because of that you got one or two people who didn't like him. The one thing with John is that if I wasn't around, no one was going to get away with anything and things would carry on as I wanted in my absence. He could get out and work with players but he was good with the injuries. It wasn't just about them lying on a table with a bit of Deep Heat to sort things out. It was about the rehabilitation, getting them up and getting them working, I knew he would work them hard. John was very honest and very reliable. He was my main sounding board.

Reserves team manager Jimmy Robson

Jimmy looked after the reserves and the kids. What a terrific guy. Extremely reliable. I still speak to him a lot. He was not only a very good coach but was a very good player who won the First Division at Burnley and played at Wembley in the FA Cup final and is the subject of a quiz question as he scored the 100th goal in a Wembley FA Cup Final. He had a very good sense of humour; he got on well with people. If someone had just had a bit of a rocket up their backside Jimmy was the guy who would have a chat with them and help them out. He never said a great deal but what he did say was very important.

Chief scout Steve Smith

Probably even quieter than Jimmy but knew what he was doing. He was responsible for bringing on the young players and to his credit, more than 20 of them went on to have long and good careers in professional football and just about all of them were local lads.

He'd just finished his playing career at Halifax when I asked him to come and train with us. We needed someone to look after the youth players so I managed to get him full-time on the payroll. Many years later after we'd had a very bad time with injuries, we were really struggling, and I only had 10 players when we were due to play Workington Town in the FA Cup and he filled in at left-back and was probably the best player on the field even though he'd not played for about five years.

Groundsman Ray Chappell

He really turned the pitch round because when I arrived it was bloody terrible. It didn't have much grass on at all but by the time I left it was one of the best in the league. If I wanted to use it during the week for a bit of work it was as if you were threatening to tread on Holy ground. Ray didn't like anyone walking on the pitch, I was the only one allowed to tread on it during the week to have a quick look at the surface. If anybody else set foot on the pitch, you'd hear a shout of 'get off my pitch' but where he came from I don't know.

Washerwoman Nellie Thompson

Nellie was the heartbeat of the club. She would be in at 6.30 every morning, everything washed and ready for training. She had a big washer and a big dryer and when we came in from training she'd come into the dressing room and take the players' kit off herself. And that's no exaggeration. She'd go in and say: 'I've seen better than that,' and get the whole bloody lot off. 'I want it in the washing machine.' Everybody had a lot of time for Nellie. She was a real character. It's people like that, who most fans won't know, who make a football club.

Maintenance man Fred Elms

Fred knew where every nook and cranny and nut and bolt were in the whole club which is understandable because he'd at the club since 1950 when he arrived with contractors to re-build the main stand and stayed for more than 40 years. He'd be there from first thing in the morning to last thing at night when he'd lock everything up. He was our odd-job man but he was vital. He had a mate who helped him. Both of them had fingers missing but neither of them ever let anything get in their way of making sure Leeds Road was a good place to work.

Grounds for concern

by former Town groundsman Ray Chappell

I was looking after the pitch at Emley when we staged a pre-season fixture against Town's first team.

The Town manager Tom Johnston saw our Welfare Ground pitch and said it was about four times better the one his team was playing on at Leeds Road.

"Why don't you come and work for us?"

"It depends on how much you're willing to pay me."

I told him how much I wanted.

"We can't pay that."

"Well I can't come then, so let's just leave it at that."

Two weeks later, Tom rang me again.

"There's no point me coming down to see you if there's no money on the table."

He'd asked the chairman to come along as well so I popped down and we came to an agreement.

He gave me what I wanted but they said they'd never paid for much for a groundsman.

"I know – and that's why it's shit. If you pay peanuts, you get monkeys like you've had on here."

I was on £100 a week which wasn't bad money but the amount of hours I put in to pull it round from being a poor pitch meant the club was getting a good deal.

They hadn't looked after it properly because they didn't know what they were doing. There were more weeds on the playing surface than grass.

If it rained heavily it used to just flood because by constantly rolling the pitch the soil became hard and the water wouldn't get soaked up.

We didn't have any tools as such because Town didn't have any money so we had to do what we could with a bit of elbow grease.

Mick Buxton took over as manager four months after I joined the club when Town were rock-bottom and Leeds Road was almost empty.

Thankfully, his team improved and the pitch got better and better and better but I would always I guard it.

At one point Mick used to let his players take a football out on to the pitch to practice but I put a stop to that.

"A pitch is for playing games on and a training pitch is for training on."

I just mentioned it once and they didn't do it again.

But if he wanted to go on and do a few set-pieces, he'd ask me and I let them because it was only right.

We needed to get better and he said that was important so I happily went down that road.

I ended up spending 24 years at Town before I retired 18 years ago and Mick's team that won the Fourth Division was really special.

They lifted everything and I really enjoyed watching them play, especially when they replaced divots during matches.

Up the Junction

Peter Fletcher

They were trying to save hard-earned cash rather than save the planet but Peter Fletcher reckons a players' car share scheme put Town on the road to glory.

Every morning before training or matches, five of the Town squad would meet up just off the M62 and squeeze into cramped second-hand cars to make their way to Leeds Road.

It seems an unlikely recipe for success as they jostled for elbow space and legroom while they trundled across the Pennines and down New Hey Road but Fletcher is certain that commuting together did the trick.

"We were always looking for ways to save a few quid because we didn't get paid that much," said Fletcher from his home in Stockport, "and that's why someone came up with the idea of a car-share – long before Peter Kay had brought out his television show."

Fletcher and his fellow travellers - Malcolm Brown, Ian Robins, Keith Hanvey and Brian Stanton - didn't need Kay's sense of humour to brighten up their journeys in those days as they had each other, a car radio and their own cassettes for a sing-along.

They would meet up just off the westbound carriageway at Milnrow, near Rochdale, and that ensured manager Mick Buxton never had to worry about his squad gelling.

"Every morning we'd have a good chat and it's because of those days that we still get on so well. The camaraderie was the best I've ever known, chatting about family life, bringing up kids, what was in the news, the football.

"We knew everyone's private lives because we'd discuss everything. That was a big plus. It meant that when you were playing you'd sweat blood for each because they were your best mates.

"We all had our own style of music with our own cassettes and we'd be singing which cheered you up even though we were tone-deaf

"Or we'd be having a good laugh and so when we arrived at work we were in the ideal frame of mind.

"It was really jovial. When we got to the club, the banter was fantastic, lots of leg pulling but nobody was hurt. If you were ganged up on you took it because you knew the next day it would be someone else's turn to get the stick.

"That's why we clicked as a team. If something bad happened to one of the lads on the field you'd be upset for them because you were so close together."

They wended their way to work back at a time when The Boomtown Rats' *I Don't Like Mondays*, Squeeze's *Up The Junction* and the Nolan Sisters' *I'm in the Mood for Dancing* were riding high in the charts.

Gary Numan's *Cars*, Pink Floyd's *Another Brick in the Wall* also hit Top of the Pops and so did, aptly, AC/DC's *Highway to Hell*.

"There were no Range Rovers, BMWs or Mercs in our car park. There were no six-bedroomed houses and there was just one car for the whole family.

"No one had a new car and we didn't have the biggest cars; they were mainly Ford Escorts, Vauxhall Vivas and small saloons.

"Malcolm had a Capri, which wasn't too bad, but with me and my small second-hand 1300 Ford Escort, trying to overtake going uphill on the M62 was a nightmare.

"We'd usually end up having to move into the inside lane with the lorries. We were scared a milk float might overtake us it was that slow and that meant we sometimes got to training late.

"What made it worse is that three of us in the car-share pool were well over six-feet tall and Ian Robins was a stocky fella so it could be uncomfortable if you were sat in the middle.

"We always got there in one piece eventually and we'd go home together and then afterwards we'd have a drink together every now and again.

"No one rushed off and the wives got close together as well

because we were all in the same boat, bringing up kids, with similar jobs."

Fletcher had previous when it came to getting lifts from his time as an apprentice at Manchester United when George Best ferried him around in his sports car.

""There were three of us that knocked about together and we'd get the bus to get to the training ground but we used to get lifts from Bestie from the training ground because we didn't have a car between us.

"Bestie had an E-type Jaguar and he'd cram in the three of us to get us back into Manchester. He was usually one of the last to leave the training ground, sitting in the shower, taking his time while we carried out our various duties and he'd give us a lift.

"There weren't empty bottles of Champagne in the car or anything like that but there was always a suitcase of spare clothing, just in case, for the next day but where he ended up we didn't know. What I do know is that he was smashing to us. There was no edge to him.

"It's funny to think we don't have any proof that we used to get lifts with George because we never took photos which is such a contrast to today with the smartphones."

Fletcher would end up in the same first-team dressing room as United legends such as Best after learning his trade in the school of hard knocks.

"It was all about school football in those days when you were a kid. I played on the street outside our two-up, two-down house in Manchester where I was brought up; playing with older boys you used to put me in goals.

"I started coming on bit-by-bit and the language of older lads pushed me to be a bit more cocky.

"In the first year of secondary school I played for the first, second and third year teams and playing with older lads, rather than just dribbling round kids your own age, brought me on leaps and bounds."

Fletcher was brought up in Openshaw (near the site of the future Etihad Stadium) before moving to West Didsbury at the age of 10.

He attended Old Moat School which became Whalley Range High School

His dad, Jim, who died in 2001, was an engineer while his mum, Olive, who is 87 and still going strong, was one of the auxiliary nurses at Withington hospital premature baby unit.

"My dad was a big influence. I remember when I was seven or eight, him chipping the ball to me, getting me to head it for hours and hours, getting me to use both feet.

"He used to take me to the park explaining things like the Stanley Matthews shuffle and at matches he'd be on the sidelines always shouting 'go with the ball' because all he was interested in was me going scoring."

His dad was a Manchester City fan who took his son to watch matches at City's old Maine Road home and Old Trafford to help him "learn as much as I could from watching the very best".

"I slacked off on education, and ended up leaving at the end of my fourth year. My mind was always on football apart from in woodwork or metalwork, which occupied my kind.

"If I'd put into maths and English what I put into football, then I'd have been an academic success but all I thought about was the game at four o'clock every day.

"Luckily for me, there was something every night to look forward and that was always in my head, I lived and breathed football.

"I could have stayed on but that was it. It was a secondary modern so you got to leave school early if you were going to be a plumber or brickie and you had a trade to get stuck into.

"I was lucky enough to be the one that became a pro footballer and if I hadn't gone down that route it would have been something on the practical side, being a plumber or joiner, rather than the brains side for me."

Fletcher had played for Manchester Boys at the age of 14 and it was at those representative games – where he faced the likes of Sam Allardyce – that talent-spotters congregated and one night a scout came to his house to invite him along to United.

"With me being a local lad, United was the one for me so I signed schoolboy forms and then at 15 signed apprentice forms, just after they'd won the European Cup.

"It was such an exciting time. When I first signed professional the three people sat opposite me were Denis Law, George Best and Paddy Crerand. Every morning you got changed you were sat listening to their conversations.

"They were big heroes but you took their company for granted. You were one of them because you were a professional. It wasn't out of the ordinary because it was just your job and you were getting with these older pros that were sat opposite you.

"There was a bit of elitism due to their age and respect but I got into the reserves they were on the edge of retiring so sometimes they'd be in the reserves and when I got to the first-team squad we were on a level par. I was one of them. You weren't in awe of anyone."

Fletcher had been signed by United manager Sir Matt Busby and can count himself as being among the last batch of Busby Babes as the Scot moved upstairs at Old Trafford shortly afterwards.

"It was awkward because he was an impossible act to follow. Wilf McGuiness and Frank O'Farrell tried to replace him and then Tommy Docherty.

"The scene was changing all the time as the old players were being whittled out and new players brought in. It was very difficult to break into a squad like that, getting into a good team that would bring you along.

"I broke into first team squad but we were relegated by Denis Law and his back-heel (for Man City) and Brian Kidd and myself were sold that year. Tommy Docherty started bringing his own players, which was his prerogative, and I was surplus to requirements and was put on the transfer list."

Fletcher made his United debut in April 1973 in a 2-2 draw at Stoke City but only made seven appearances before he was the £36,000 "makeweight" in a deal that saw him swap places with Hull striker Stuart Pearson.

"Terry Neill was the manager at Hull and he said this, that and the other but I'd been there two months and he cleared his desk and went to Spurs. And so I had to prove myself to a new boss and you're not always their cup of tea."

He spent two years at Boothferry Park before moving to Stockport where he spent another two seasons and then Town manager Tom Johnston made an approach.

"I'd had a couple of clubs in for me but I fancied Huddersfield because it had the history of a big club but it had fallen on hard times so the prospects were good.

"Tom rang me up. I told him I was supposed to be going to Wigan and he told me to ring them up and come to Huddersfield because they'd definitely offer me terms to sign on so I called Wigan and drove to Huddersfield for a chat with him and signed on the dotted line."

His Huddersfield career began in earnest on the opening day of the 1978/79 season with a 0-0 draw against Crewe in front of 2,838 as the locals voted with their feet but he benefited from Buxton's promotion.

"We got fitter and Mick made us realise what we could achieve and when you realise there's something at the end of it then it created a buzz. It snowballed when we were winning. We were on a roll, you were confident and anything was possible.

"I hit it off with Ian Robins when he came in and there was the tall and the short, different styles. It worked a treat. It was telepathic. You anticipate things and we were sharing the goals.

"I was nearly 6ft 2in so I always had a chance in the air and scored my fair share of headers. For a big fella I thought I had good feet and always wanted to get involved in the build-up, I dropped back to help midfield and leave Robbo on his own and then when we attacked I'd push up as a twin two."

Fletcher had scored 13 league goals when he lost his place in the team due to Kindon's arrival but there was no sense of injustice.

"It was a surprise that Mick got Kindo but he had a great impact. His enthusiasm, jovial nature and size may have intimidated some people but because of how we got to know him he was good for the changing room.

"He'd gee us up and his experience helped us over the finishing line. The fans really took to him and the players did too.

"On a personal level, it might have been a Godsend for me that Mick brought in someone else because it gave me a break

"It probably helped my progression because I was struggling with my back and my ankles, which had to strapped up every day before training by John Haselden.

"I'd had two very weak ankles all my life with being so tall and as a young chap going to Manchester boys I'd gone over on my ankles and then my back problems started. They might have been connected.

"If I'd been healthy and fully fit and not getting in when things weren't going well, I'd have been more annoyed or frustrated but it was just one of those things. I sort of accepted it and that was probably pleasing for Mick that I wasn't banging on his door."

Fletcher ended up playing a crucial role in the run-in with the two goals that cemented promotion in a 3-1 at Hereford and another in the penultimate game, a 4-2 win over Torquay at Leeds Road.

"A few were concerned for me as pals and that was okay and the other lads may have felt sorry for me but sympathy would have been secondary to them playing.

"I still felt involved as sub. I came on and scored so I got the adulation. It gave me a lift. It wasn't just being twelfth man.

"But what honestly kept me focused was the prospect of doing my bit to help that group of lads, who'd hardly won a thing, to enjoy a bit of glory. We'd played for years and years but never had anything tangible to show for it.

"It was such a relief when Robbo got those goals against Hartlepool but I knew we'd get there in the end.

"My family came over to Huddersfield when we had our big civic reception with the fans on the Town Hall balcony. They were in awe. It was like we were FA Cup winners. It was a dream come true for such a small squad of lads."

....

Slowly but surely, Peter Fletcher's football career tapered off after Town won the Fourth Division.

He was unable to kick a ball the year after helping Town to silverware due to injury problems and a 2-0 defeat at Lincoln City in April 1982 marked his final game in blue and white stripes.

"Even when I was over at Hull, I'd have a dull ache in my back and I'd go into the club for heat treatment to help me play through the pain.

"The bottom disc had worn and I used to miss training and then I went to see specialists in Manchester and Harley Street who decided the disc needed trimming off and off I went for surgery at Leeds Royal Infirmary.

"I resumed training but after a several months I went home one day and I couldn't lift my leg.

"I was sent down to Harley Street and they said I'd done well to get where I was in football but if I pursued my career any further I'd end up with a permanent limp."

Fletcher was advised to call it a day and find another job.

"That's when reality kicked in and I had to see Mick and my contract was finished with Huddersfield Town. It suddenly ground to a halt and that's why, to this day, the title win was so important.

"Unfortunately, I hadn't prepared for life after football. It's naïve but you think you'll play until you're 50. I'd not looked that far ahead and I thought I'd have plenty of time to sort something out.

"I was upset that I'd taken no coaching badges and had two children and a wife (Margaret) to support and there was not a lot I could do after Town. I was on the sick for five months because my back was so bad."

The father-of-three ended up getting back on his own two feet and landed a local authority job in Stockport, working in security for almost 30 years and becoming a supervisor before retiring at the age of 60 with five grandchildren to keep him busy.

"There's also something to do whether it's taking grandkids swimming, gardening, seeing people and socialising, or now looking forward to watching Town play Man United."

Town's best ever Christmas present

Steve Kindon

Steve Kindon stood up and paced around the damp and dank dressing room with its whitewashed walls.

His new Huddersfield Town teammates watched as Kindon tried to make sense of his strange surroundings in the lower reaches of the Football League.

He had gone from rubbing shoulders English football's finest on marble corridors steeped in history to fighting for elbow room in Spartan changing facilities on Boxing Day 1979.

"Is this a fucking dressing room?" Kindon said to his new Town colleagues. "Well, it's fuck-all like Highbury."

It is thanks to his decision to join Town in December 1979 that he completed an unlikely journey from renowned stages like Arsenal's Highbury stadium to The Shay ground, home to Town's local rivals Halifax.

Kindon was reflecting on his fall from grace over coffee on the patio of pub with a packet of cigarettes on the table on the outskirts of Bristol.

"I like to take the piss out of myself and they all burst into laughter when I said that. It broke the ice."

The raconteur was in-between the after-dinner speaking engagements which now enable him to make a healthy living, judging by the Mercedes with its personalised number plate.

"My first game was at Halifax and for no good reason I was sat next to Keith Hanvey on the bus and I followed him in through the players' entrance and turned into this room with its whitewashed walls and benches.

"Keith started to take his jacket and tie off and I told him not to bother yet but to hang on till we got into the dressing room. 'But this is the fucking dressing room,' he said.

"My initial thought was: 'What the fuck have I done,' I meant no disrespect but at Arsenal, like American football teams, each player had a little cubicle with individual coat hangers.

"It was the same at Aston Villa, Manchester United and City. That was my heritage and we ended up in this pokey little cubicle with whitewashed walls. You had to laugh."

It was not the best of starts but for Kindon, who was the substitute that cold winter's day in Halifax, it was about to get worse.

"The Shay being The Shay they had a speedway track around the pitch and the trainers' dugouts, which were heavy wooden boxes for three or four people, were positioned inside it, 20 yards or so away from the stand.

"The lads normally ran out in tracksuits tops and it was my job, as sub, to gather them in but because it was bitterly cold they wore bottoms as well so I was heavily laden.

"Just when I got to the trainers' dugout the blasted thing blew over. I put the kit down and tried to pick it up, battling against the wind and there was a policeman just stood there a few yards away – 'Don't fucking help will you?' – and he laughed his head off at me.

"I had to leave it there and two minutes later John (Haselden) and Mick (Buxton) came out smelling of whisky and leant a hand. I thought to myself – this wouldn't happen at Old Trafford. It wouldn't even happen at Turf Moor."

Town lost 2-1 that day despite a cameo role from Kindon, who still insists he should have been credited with the goal rather than Halifax defender Chris Dunleavy "as he staggered back to goal".

Kindon certainly made an instant impression on *Huddersfield Daily Examiner* reporter Paul Clark.

"We knew almost instantly that 'Kindo' was the perfect Christmas present. He was an irresistible force in the second half of the season as the Terriers stormed to the Fourth Division championship.

"Who can forget that display of menacing power before he made his Boxing Day debut at Halifax and that was only on The Shay trackside as he warmed up?"

Warrington-born Kindon was familiar to Buxton from their days together on Burnley's books.

He had been transfer-listed during his second spell at Turf Moor after returning from Wolves because, he was told "the chairman (Bob Lord) said I was earning too much money".

Buxton launched a charm offensive but Kindon twice rejected his advances before eventually agreeing to move in a £40,000-deal that was signed, sealed and delivered late into the night after a home game.

"Mick came to my house twice with George Binns (Town's secretary). He told me: 'As much as you're thought of at Burnley you'll be as well thought of at Huddersfield, you'd the catalyst to get us up and you'd be a hero for life.'

"He couldn't afford what I was on at Burnley, which was a king's ransom but he upped the wage offered originally but I turned him down.

"I phoned my old manager at Wolves, Billy McGarry, who used to play for Town, and Sammy Cheung, and people I respected and every single one of them advised me against going to Town.

"They said that because Town were in the Fourth Division, most centre-backs would just want to kick me for fun, especially if you're going in there with first division pedigree. It was a case of I'll show him."

Curiosity got the better of Kindon who headed over to Huddersfield and paid to watch Town demolish Rochdale 5-1 one wet and windy Friday night.

"I just wanted to get a taste of the atmosphere and a feel for the stadium. I sat down and some people recognised me and said 'you're just what we need – an old head' and I thought 'fuck off I was 28 only last week'."

Town were on song and Kindon saw enough to have a change of heart. He headed to Buxton's office and Binns was beckoned to complete the paperwork on the deal late that night. "George would say that I was the best Christmas present the club had ever had."

Reserves team manager Jimmy Robson got in on the act the following morning when he drove over to the Football League headquarters in Lytham St Anne's to make sure Kindon was registered in time for the festive period.

It represented a major coup for Buxton at a club where the biggest fee forked out for a player was the £65,000 to Manchester United for striker Alan Gowling's services June 1972.

"I wanted someone who would light the place up and get the fans thinking 'bloody hell'," Buxton said. "I said to the chairman (Keith Longbottom), Steve Kindon would put about 5,000 on the gate and you'd get your money back pronto. That's how I managed to convince the board."

Kindon, who had been crowned 'Fastest Footballer in Britain' in 1976 at a event at Edinburgh's Meadowbank Stadium organised by Ladbrokes, would hit the ground running.

He took the Fourth Division by storm with swashbuckling forward play but only after his new teammates got a taste of things to come.

"It was in one of the first training sessions, I got on the wrong side of our very own version of Roy Keane, our skipper Peter Hart who talks very gently these days because he's a vicar but he was our hard man.

"We had this game where there'd be seven or eight lads on each side who were all numbered and John Haselden called out numbers and we had to run out and play two a side and score a goal. It was very intense.

"I sprinted out. I was very fast and got there yards before Peter, shielded the ball, stuck out my arm and I not so much as broke his nose but splattered it but it was a complete accident.

"Training stopped, blood was spurting all over the pace. Micky Laverick broke the silence: 'Did you see that? It was very clever because he's a First Division player. He knows all the tricks of the trade.' Thankfully, Peter didn't hold a grudge."

While most Town fans revered Kindon, it was difficult not to have sympathy for Peter Fletcher who made way for the marquee signing despite forming such a potent partnership with Ian Robins and yet Kindon feels no remorse.

"You say 'it wasn't broke, so why fix it?' but we were in sixth when I arrived although we had every chance of winning promotion.

"I didn't owe Peter an apology, plus it ended up being money for old rope for him because he was substitute for about 20 games which meant he was on first-team money without playing.

"And it wasn't an elephant in the room; it's what you do. Someone will have taken Peter's place at Manchester United where he played half-a-dozen games and then he'll have taken someone else's place at Town.

"I'm not saying that everyone's mercenary but if you're on five grand a week at Huddersfield, however much you love the club, if someone offers you 20 grand a week to play elsewhere, you'll go. We're all transitory.

"As a mercenary I went back to Burnley and then as a freelancer, wanting to earn my wage, I wanted to play for Huddersfield Town and I wanted to do the best I could for Huddersfield Town. And in my opinion I happened to be a better player than Peter Fletcher and a better player than Ian Robins. It's their fault if they can't keep up."

Kindon may have replaced a popular figure but it didn't take the bustling striker long to win over fans and players alike.

"I've always been a team player. My dad was in the Army and he taught me important values and I grew up playing rugby at grammar school (he earned eight O-levels at Wade Deacon School, Widnes) which is more of a team sport than soccer.

"Some people find it difficult to settle into new surroundings but I'm not one of them. I just gel with people. I've kept in touch with all the Burnley lads I grew up with, the Wolves lads I played with and all the Huddersfield lads.

"I was enthusiastic; I worked hard. I was the captain without being captain. I was the gobby one: 'Pick him up, Brian work back,' I never stopped talking for 90 minutes but apparently I was well liked by them and highly respected.

"I was always the out-ball. If they were struggling it was a case of 'play it into the corner, Kindo will catch it'. My home debut epitomised the way I went about my work, my modus operandi.

"It was a frosty pitch, against Darlington, we went out in flat-soled trainers. Early on they played the ball over my head towards the open end to the far left-hand corner.

"Their right-back had a 15-yard start on me and I just kept it in play and everyone in the terrace gave me a cheer and started chanting 'Kindon, Kindon, Kindon' which meant I'd won them over very quickly. First impressions count at lot."

What fans didn't witness were the obsessively well-organised Kindon's quirky pre-match habits behind the scenes.

"In football you've got a pair of undies that you call your 'slip'. I always put my left leg in first and it was the same with my shorts and socks and my boots and then I'd tie my left boot first. I always favoured my left foot. Now when I get dressed I still put my left leg in my undies first and so on.

"When I was at Wolves they nicknamed me the 'Tank', we signed Willie Carr for big money and there was a photo taken on his debut and I was just in front of him going out and we won 7-1.

"It was the best game of my career at Molineux and right at the bottom of a match report the day it said: 'Wolves have bought a Carr for the rest of the season but this game was won by a tank.' Wherever we went afterwards, I always nipped just in front of Willie but I never played as well again."

Kindon can hardly remember Buxton the player but he left an indelible impression on him as a "deep-thinker" of a manager and an evening game at Exeter has special significance.

Kindon was in the dressing room waiting for a 7.30pm kick off when he was summoned by Buxton, told to forget about putting on boots and led down the players' tunnel.

'Steven, what do you see over there behind the goal?'

"I looked and saw our own fans and he said there were two or three thousand Town supporters.

'Those lads love you. You've not been scoring. You've been playing great but you've gone a little bit shot-shy – you're laying it off too much.

'I want you to do one thing for me tonight and that's to score a goal for me.

'If you score a goal for me tonight then we'll win this game.

"I scored a goal early on and the lads were trying to jump on me but I ran to the dugout and said 'that's for you boss'.

"Ten minutes later I scored another and ran straight to the dugout again and said that's for the fans boss.

"And then I got my hat-trick and ran to Mick Buxton again and said that one's for me."

"The point I'm making is that Mick knew how to get the best out of me. It was an arm round the shoulder and ask me nicely to score a goal. It was the same with people like Ian Robins.

"I like to be mothered so I gave everything back to the crowd that I could. Those chants of 'Kindon, Kindon, Kindon,' meant a lot to me. They might not have mattered to others so much."

Unlike Buxton, Town coach Robson had made a big impression on Kindon when they were both at Burnley.

"Jimmy told me football mirrors life. There's no such thing as black and white.

"You can lose 10-0 and it's not totally black if you got a couple of corners and work on what you did to earn those corners.

"You can win 10-0 and it's not all white because they got a couple of corners and you need to work on preventing those corners.

"Life's the same. There are only shades of grey. You often learn more from a 2-0 defeat than a 2-0 win.

"After a win you go and have a beer in the bar but lose and you start analysing what went wrong. I was about 18. I don't forget pearls of wisdom like that."

The England Youth international put the advice to good use. He played 120 times for the Clarets before a £100,000 move to Wolves in July 1972 before returning to Burnley five years later in an £80,000 deal.

Kindon would provide that spark that gave Town the edge over

Walsall and he put his experience to good use on and off the field as the finishing line in the title race loomed.

A fortnight before the end of the season, Kindon called a team meeting and proved he was ready to put his money where his mouth was.

His business acumen also showed why he would become Town's commercial manager after he was forced to quit football due to a knee injury in May 1982 after scoring 37 goals in 82 Town games.

"I said: 'Lads we've got a great chance of winning the title. If we're champions we'll have lots of financial opportunities – the press will want interviews and businessmen in town will want us to open supermarkets and show off new cars and the like.

"So I suggested we formed a players' committee and all the money gets pooled and distributed equally so we're all getting an even share. I did it because in 1974 at Wolves I was part of the pool, I got injured and never got a share.

"Chris Topping was the only one to pick up on what I was doing.

'Are you sure about that Steven?'

'Yes, why?'

'Because you'd be the one who has to open that supermarket and you'll be the one who gets interviewed so it's very generous of you to share all your money with us.

'But the team's got us so far and the team will get us over the line so let's split it 16 ways. It was the right thing to go."

For once, though, Kindon was unable to take a game by the scruff of the neck when Town faced Hartlepool with the Fourth Division title on the line.

"I wasn't influential. I was peripheral. We came in at half-time, losing 1-0 and Mick told us we just had to keep going. I was convinced we were too good not to win.

"The game changed when all of a sudden we got 90 per cent of the possession and pressure and it turned into a game played almost entirely in the Hartlepool half which didn't suit me. I wanted space behind the defenders.

"It would have suited Peter much more but Robbo came to the rescue. The timing of his runs, his control was superb and his goals were invaluable. We couldn't have gone up as champions that year without him.

"Winning the title meant a lot to me. It wasn't small beer. There were 92 Football League clubs and just seven trophies to be won and 24 teams were all vying to be Fourth Division champions."

Once the celebrations had died down, Kindon and his teammates would return to Leeds Road for one last time before heading off on holiday.

"We were told to report for an 11am team photo-call and as we walked down the tunnel, Keith Hanvey stopped me. I wondered what was up.

'It's the first time I've run down this tunnel in six months without hearing the crowd going 'Kindon, Kindon, Kindon,'

"The name of Kindon became the team chant for the season as we ran out. That was some compliment."

....

Hartlepool will always have a special place in Town's history because of the events of May 3, 1979.

But it was a trip up to Pools' Victoria Ground on the North Sea coast and a duel with their centre-half, Billy Ayre, that has a permanent place in Steve Kindon's football memories.

"One of my first Town games was up at Hartlepool and I was gob-smacked because Mick called me into his office and said there's a centre-half you're going to be up against called Billy Ayre and he's a mad man.

"Mick said 'I'll never say this to you again but if there's a 50-50 let him have it because I've bought you for the season to get us up and I don't want you getting injured.'

"Then on the Tuesday or Wednesday, we were warming up for training, I saw Robbo (Ian Robins) and Fletch (Peter Fletcher) and

went over for a chat.

'All right lads?'

'Just thinking, Saturday we're up against Billy Ayre.'

'Who's this Billy Ayre?

'He's a nutter.'

"*I went shopping in town and got talking to some fans.*

'It's Billy Ayre on Saturday.'

'Yes I fucking know it is.'

"*I was wondering: who is this monster?*

"*Come the Saturday, I was warming up with Andy Rankin when Hartlepool came out.*

"*Someone shouted at me – 'Kindon - none of your fancy-Dan First Division tricks today - I'm gonna do you.'*

"*And he ran off, I looked at Andy – who was as dry as they came – and he quipped 'intelligent conversation was it?'*

"*It must have been Billy Ayre. It got me thinking about what Mick had said, him wanting me for the rest of the season.*

"*But did I follow his instructions? Did I fuck.*"

According to Kindon, they "battered each other to death" but attack became the best form of defence for the Town striker.

"*Andy didn't have a long kick and as we were playing into the wind the ball went up and came down vertically and I knew this is the obvious opportunity for me to take a whack.*

"*I jumped as though to head it but I jumped to the side and went whack. And there was this monster Billy Ayre just trying to head the ball, not trying to do me at all and I caught him across the face.*

"*He collapsed and it was horrible of me to do. The nine Hartlepool players should have steamed into me but all I heard was 'fucking hell he's done Billy' so I went up in their esteem.*

"*For 90 minutes we kicked each other. Fairly. We hurt each other fairly. We walked off afterwards like soldiers battered and bruised with arms around each other.*

'See you in 20 minutes for a beer, Kindo.'

'Too right.'

On that final day of the season there was knock on Town's dressing room door. It was Billy Ayre.

'Kindo – hope you do it today…..but I'm not going to help you'.

"That was everything I would have wanted, hoped for and expected of him."

Saving the best till last

Ian Robins

If he casts his mind back, Ian Robins can still paint a vivid picture of the dramatic events just after four o'clock on Saturday, May 3, 1980.

Robins still remembers the unlikely sight of centre-back Keith Hanvey galloping down the wing ahead of his equaliser against Hartlepool at Leeds Road.

And he still remembers half-an-hour or so later taking advantage of the chaos that ensued after the Mitre match ball had cannoned off the crossbar following Peter Hart's long throw-in and dropped invitingly into the dusty six-yard box.

But what still really stands out is the re-collection of leaping to his feet after scoring again and charging straight towards the Cowshed to lead the celebrations with the Town fans in a 16,807-strong crowd.

It was the most important goal of his life and his side's 101st goal of the League campaign.

Robins had put Town on course to be crowned Fourth Division champions and in doing so ensured his team's place in Town folklore.

And it was his instinctive reaction to share the most special of moments with the club's supporters.

A clenched-fist salute to the Cowshed and jig of joy said it all after he had stooped to conquer and sealed what proved to be an unassailable 2-1 lead for Town as time ebbed away on the final day of the season.

"The Hartlepool game will always stand out for me because it was a great, great, great occasion on a great, great, great day," Robins said from his Wigan home.

"The atmosphere was phenomenal. It was a bit jittery but the whole place ended up bouncing.

"I usually celebrated with the lads first if I scored but I went straight to the Cowshed first because we'd had great support, home and away.

"Loads travelled everywhere and made a right racket wherever went. It was a way of saying 'thank you' for supporting us all season.

"In those days fans were closer to the action than they are now at modern grounds. That's why we had such a special bond with the fans and the fans had a bond with us. It was the perfect way to finish it. I was just thinking: 'We've got there.'"

It turned out to be a jubilant occasion for Town but it could have been so different had it not been for Robins' heroics.

"It was a funny old day. It was a massive game and we knew there was so much riding on it. Sometimes you're not aware of how bad you're playing or what you're doing wrong until someone tells you which is what Mick did.

"He said we were losing because we weren't playing as a team. We weren't playing as we could. He challenged us to put things right in the dressing room at half-time and we did do.

"We went out and played some brilliant stuff. It was as if it was meant to be that we'd score the winning goals in front of the Cowshed. It felt like destiny."

It was left to Robins to come to the rescue as Town faltered with his headers in one of the most exciting days in the history of Leeds Road and he remembers the drama unfolding as if it was yesterday.

"To this day, I still don't know what on earth Keith Hanvey was doing charging down the wing to cross the ball for the first goal.

"He was always up for set-pieces but I'd never even seen Keith get over the half-way line with the ball at his feet. I'm so glad he had his little rush of blood to the head and took things into his own hands because he got a great cross in for me to duck down and head in.

"We were all over them and time was running out but I knew I'd get a chance sooner or later because we were wearing down them. We were all over them. I just had to bide my time.

"There wasn't long left when the ball bounced off the crossbar after a long throw by Peter Hart and I just happened to be in the right place at the right time and all I had to do was dive forward to head it in again.

"It was a brilliant feeling because Mick had built a very good team and we'd worked really hard that season. I knew that was an icing-on-the-cake sort of finish. Not many teams ever score 100 or more goals."

It had taken a huge leap of faith from Robins to take the plunge to join nose-diving Town and secure a special niche in club history.

Robins had been a midfielder when Mick Buxton visited his Lancashire home and asked him to drop down the leagues and become a striker.

Anyone who saw Town as they charged up the divisions will know it turned out to be an inspired move, as Robins became certainly the first and arguably most important signing of Buxton's Town tenure.

A player of Robins' ilk – strong and stock and ready to lead Town's attack - was crucial to Buxton's vision of the brave new world at Leeds Road.

He was not only key to build-up play all season as Buxton re-shaped tactics, but his goal-poaching abilities proved dreams do come true for Terriers supporters long before Wembley play-off final hero Christopher Schindler was even born.

"I'd started off initially as a striker at Oldham but then went into midfield there and at Bury but then Mick wanted to turn me back into a centre-forward because he thought I could hold the ball up well.

"Mick clearly saw something in me that others couldn't. It took me by surprise but I let my head rule my heart. That's because I got the feeling I could trust Mick and I was proved right because I had the time of my life at Town.

"I'd not played up front for a good while but I just thought: 'Okay, why not, no problem.' I didn't really fancy having to travel over the Pennines every day but I got the impression that Mick would put his money where his mouth was."

But Buxton not only had to convince his priority transfer target to move but also his wife, Elaine, which is why he jumped in his car and drove over to meet them both.

"Somebody at Bury told me to get over to Huddersfield because they're interested in signing you so the first thing I did was ring our Elaine to tell her what was going on.

"It had to be a joint-decision between Elaine and me. You can't make a decision and then just come home and say 'by the way, love, I've just signed for a new club'. It wouldn't have been appropriate.

"It was important she had her say and she had her reservations about Huddersfield: 'Hold on you're going from second to third to fourth'.

"She had a good point because I'd been playing against the likes of Bobby Moore and George Best when they were in the Second Division with Fulham so I wasn't sure. I meant no disrespect to the players but it felt like I was having to get in on another re-building job like I'd done at Oldham.

"I thought 'blooming heck, I'm going downhill here at a rapid rate of knots' so I was reluctant to join Town at first. That's why Mick came across to our house to have a word with me and my missus and persuade us that it would be the best thing I could do.

"Mick was pretty forceful and seemed like he was the sort of person who knew what he was talking about. He spoke about what ambitions he had for the club and then we decided between us that I'd sign."

Robins told Buxton he would "give it a go" and believes the decision paid off "because everyone clicked thanks to Mick."

"He was clever at getting the very best from every player. He had a plan for every one of us. It was like we were all pieces in a game of chess. Mick would manoeuvre you around according to what he wanted you to do.

"Mick said he wanted us to be the start of a new generation. I'd been unsure whether I fancied the challenge but it turned out to be the best football decision I ever made."

After joining Town from Oldham for £20,000 in September 1978, Robins scored 16 goals in 38 Fourth Division games in his maiden campaign in his new position.

But he was just getting warmed up as he was not only the lynchpin of Buxton's attack the following season but he also helped himself to 25 League goals.

He was officially the Fourth Division's top scorer although former Town striker Colin Garwood could beg to differ as he was leading scorer for both Portsmouth (17 in 24 games) and Aldershot (10 in 16).

Robins, who was born in Bury, had shown he was destined for good things as a youngster and was the toast of East Ward Secondary Modern School as he represented England schoolboys.

He caught the eye of Oldham scouts while scoring a hat-trick for his Sunday league side and signed on straight after leaving school when Burnley legend Jimmy McIlroy was manager at Boundary Park and Ken Bates was chairman.

He made his debut in 1969 two years after signing apprenticeship forms and helped the Latics rise from Fourth to Second Division before moving to Bury in a £25,000-deal in July 1977 and playing all but one game the following season for a side that struggled in the Third Division.

"Bury didn't work out for me because we had Bob Stokoe as manager and I went in one day and he told me Huddersfield had put a bid in for me so would I drive across and speak to Mr Buxton?

"It helped that I already knew about Town because of Les Chapman from our time at Oldham. It was ridiculous a club of Huddersfield's stature was in the Fourth Division.

"So I always knew Huddersfield Town was a big club but it just needed a spark to bring it back to life and that's what Mick Buxton provided. He started Huddersfield's revival after years of mismanagement."

Town chairman Keith Longbottom sanctioned the £20,000 signing of Robins.

"We weren't on ridiculous amounts of money in those days. But then again it wasn't about the money – it was about playing the game. Nobody was hung up on the money we earned.

"I was on about £35 a week when I was at Oldham and I topped that up with bonuses and when I went to Huddersfield I was getting decent money but it's nothing proportion-wise compared to what players get nowadays."

His first car was a second-hand Ford Cortina followed by a Vauxhall Viva while the newly-wed Robins also bought their first home together, a £7,500 three-bedroomed semi-detached house in Wigan.

"There were no agents or hangers-on to be seen anywhere near the club. I'm a bit old-fashioned but I don't really think I'd have wanted an agent to negotiate deals and get me better money because if you can't sort out your own destiny then there's something wrong.

"We never had big houses. There was no Sky Sports in those days. Their big TV money wasn't in the game then and you were lucky if you saw football on the telly apart from the home internationals or England in the World Cup. There was Match of the Day but they only had the highlights.

"We had our holidays in Abersoch where we hired a caravan or got a chalet for the whole family and we always had a great time – whatever the weather. We didn't go overseas much. If you went abroad you had to be rich which we weren't."

After his annual visit to the Welsh seaside resort, Robins received "a nice warm welcome from people like Keith Hanvey" at Town before throwing himself into pre-season training.

"Mick was a really hard taskmaster but it was part and parcel of his grand plan so we all got on with it.

"Training generally could be horrible but pre-season was hellish. We'd go for runs on the hills around Huddersfield. It was hard graft. They didn't pull any punches.

"It was okay for people like Mick Laverick and Brian Stanton who had hearts and lungs and legs like Mo Farah and could run all day but I was better off with the short, 50-metre stuff.

"I didn't like the long runs because I didn't find them inspiring. I preferred to have the ball at my feet, seeing the ball hit the back of the net.

"There was a time I went AWOL on a run. I'd been somewhere and couldn't find where they were.

"It was raining hard and I hid in this bush and waited for them to come round and then suddenly appeared from nowhere to join in with them. They all thought I was a shirker but it was a one-off."

It may have been the '70s but Town's staff were on the ball as far as health and diet were concerned.

"I know sports science is a big thing now and there's lot of information about nutrition. In our day, you'd just get weighed every Friday to make sure we were on the straight and narrow.

"But we always watched what we ate. For pre-match meals we had scrambled or poached egg on toast or beans on toast, light meals. In the morning we had breakfast with lots of oats and fruit in, like granola.

"There were none of the energy drinks there are today for footballers. Back then Lucozade was wrapped in yellow cellophane and was just for visiting people in hospital."

Despite an amicable Yorkshire-Lancashire divide in the playing ranks, Robins fondly remembers a "tremendous sense of togetherness."

"They used to call us the Lancashire Mob because we travelled in together and played in the seven-a-sides together.

"Everyone had second-hand cars. Ford Cortinas or Escorts or a Ford Capri and Malcolm Brown had the flashiest. There'd be five of us in a car. Imagine that nowadays? They'd probably arrive in a helicopter.

"Sometimes at football clubs you get people who don't like each other but we all got on. There was no backbiting. Prima donnas wouldn't have lasted.

"We were a band of brothers. If you hit one of us, you hit all of us. We were well drilled. Everybody knew what was required of them.

"It was a case of 'get the ball, get it forward as quickly as you can – without hoofing it - and get someone on the end of it'. It wasn't rocket science.

"It was my responsibility to get hold of the ball, play other people in and put the ball in the back of the net.

"I didn't know whether to laugh or cry when Harry Kane took free-kicks in the European Championships even though he was England's main striker. I never took set-pieces. It was my job to convert them."

Goals came thick and fast for Robins but the 7-1 win over Port Vale stands out as the "best team display of the season". "It was amazing. We'd have beaten most teams in England that day. We were virtually invincible."

Town went from strength to strength as the season progressed.

"We were good to watch and fans responded by paying to come and see us. That was the ultimate seal of approval and we had a good bond with local people.

"We had loyalty towards each other and to our club. Now players have their agents and when they don't get things their own way they spit the dummies out."

That was anything but the case as Robins, Steve Kindon and Peter Fletcher competed for the two forward slots and all chipped in with vital goals as the season approached a dramatic finale but it was Robins who had the final say.

"When I first signed there were crowds of just a few thousand so to win the title in front of almost 17,000 fans just showed how far we'd come in a relatively short space of time."

....

It was a huge surprise to everyone connected with Huddersfield Town when Ian Robins announced his retirement just two years after his goals clinched the Fourth Division title.

Now, for the first time, Robins has spoken publicly about the tragic family circumstances that lay behind his decision to bring to a halt a career that yielded 104 goals in 424 Football League games.

"It was the worst day of my life. It was pre-season and my father-in-

law (Arthur Pilkington) came across to our house and when he arrived he collapsed and died of a heart attack right in front of me.

"I was in the garden and he slumped to the floor at the back gate. He probably died there and then. I called an ambulance and went with him to hospital and about 10 minutes later they pronounced him dead.

"Elaine was expecting our second child and was at the local maternity unit having tests and so I had to go there by taxi and speak to her and my mother-in-law and deliver the bad news."

It was as they came to terms with the family tragedy that Robins called time on his career at the age of 30.

"There was lots of soul-searching for me but I came to the conclusion that family needed me more than Huddersfield Town.

"I just felt family came before football. Our daughter was very young and our son on the way and we were in bits over Arthur who was a great father-in-law.

"All of sudden football just didn't seem as important to me as family and I thought if I'm going to finish I'm going to finish at a club where I love being.

"It wasn't that I'd had enough of football because I was having the best time of my career.

"It was that Elaine was just a couple of months from having our second baby and I just decided that as much as I loved football and Huddersfield that family came before that."

Robins, who is now 65 and still active "pottering around" in the world of business, bought a newsagents in Wigan and then went into managing a sales team with a Lancashire company called Port Petroleum.

"I could have stayed in football and gone on somewhere else but I didn't want to go anywhere else even when Wigan asked me to join them.

"I've got no regrets. Looking back I still feel I made the right decision but I never lost my feelings towards Huddersfield Town – the club will always be in my heart and in my soul."

Town's title – but it's not a champion show

Monday, May 5, 1980

Town 2 Hartlepool 1

Match report

Their finest hour – but their worst performance of the season.

That one short sentence neatly encapsulates Saturday's title show at Leeds Road, which brought the curtain down for the last time.

Yes, Town are rightfully champions of the Fourth Division but the ultimate accolade was captured with a struggle not a swagger.

That may appear a trifle churlish but Mick Buxton's heroes were never allowed to turn on the style in the way that has devastated so many teams since last August.

Hartlepool's unflinching devotion to spoiling the championship party made sure of that.

Their barn-door defence was securely bolted and Town laboured in their efforts to break it down.

The match, though, was never going to be a classic for the strong wind – which Buxton later admitted he had underestimated – was a major influence.

It was erratic and swirling and played hideous tricks with the flight of the ball.

Town, however, despite the hostile conditions and Hartlepool's resolve came from a goal down to win.

The result, as the Town chief admitted to me afterwards, was "all that mattered".

"I always like to play well and win but it's nice to play lousy for once and still win," he said. "That was our worst display of the season."

The worst or not, it was, in the final analysis, good enough to beat Hartlepool.

The story and anguish that followed might have been so different if Town had taken the lead after just three minutes.

Peter Fletcher hurtled towards a Steve Kindon cross but goalkeeper Graham Richardson blocked the header and sent the striker sprawling as the two men collided.

A goal then would have signaled a tremendous flourish but Town never settled into a convincing or penetrative rhythm.

Hartlepool, with three centre-backs casting as big a shadow over Town's efforts as the main stand, also broke dangerously and twice Derek Hampton's left foot reminded Leeds Road that the visitors could play a bit as well.

After 22 minutes, Ian Robins dropped a header on to the roof of Richardson's net and on the half-hour the goalkeeper rescued his side when Bernard Purdie seemed poised to score his first ever goal for the club.

Richardson smothered the ball at Purdie's feet and the save was a prelude to Hartlepool taking the lead after 38 minutes.

John Linacre, who missed the team coach earlier in the morning and motored down the A1 himself, showed somewhat better timing on the pitch.

Keith Hanvey's tackle halted Hampton's progress on the edge of the penalty area but as the ball spun free, Linacre lofted it wide of Andy Rankin.

A hushed Leeds Road broke its silence as Purdie engineered another forward sortie but seconds before the interval that man Hampton connected nicely with a low shot, the ball skidding wide of Rankin's right-hand post.

Town resumed with Dave Cowling replacing a concussed Dave Sutton – "I felt as though I'd been hit by a brick and there was no way I could carry on," he said later – and Peter Hart switching to the centre of the defence.

Within an instant, though – for the statisticians the precise time was

47min 12sec – Town were level and the fans were saluting the team's 100th goal of the campaign.

Hanvey powered down the right, nodded the bouncing ball forward and continued his charge towards the byline where he whipped the ball across the face of the Hartlepool goal.

From within a forest of legs, Robins plunged headlong to direct it over the line and he emerged triumphant from a confused cluster of bodies.

Cowling, who swiftly began to stamp his authority in midfield, twice went close to scoring while Hampton – who else? – could have restored Hartlepool's lead in the 67th minute when Rankin palmed Linacre's corner straight to his feet.

Finally, with nine minutes remaining, and Walsall trailing to a rampant Newport, Town went in front.

Another prodigious throw from Hart propelled the ball on to the head of defender Steve Brooks who unwittingly guided it on the crossbar. With Richardson grasping air, Robins dispatched the ball beyond him with customary aplomb.

....

Twelve months earlier Town had been beaten 2-0 by Hartlepool in the penultimate game of the season.

Now they were set to end eight years of heartache during which the club had dropped from the top flight to the basement division.

Although promotion to Division III had already been clinched manager Mick Buxton desperately wanted his side to take the Fourth Division title and top the century of league goals.

MATCH VERDICT
Melvyn Booth

Town's title — but it's not a champion show

THEIR finest hour ... but their worst performance of the season.

That one short sentence neatly capsules Saturday's title show at Leeds Road which brought the curtain down for the last time.

Yes, Town are rightfully champions of the Fourth Division, but the ultimate accolade was captured with a struggle not a swagger.

That may appear a trifle churlish, but Mick Buxton's heroes were never allowed to turn on the style that has devastated so many teams since last August.

Hartlepool's unflinching devotion to spoiling the championship party made sure of that.

Their barn door defence was securely bolted and Town laboured in their efforts to break it down.

The match, though, was never going to be a classic, for the strong wind — which Buxton later admitted he had underestimated — was a major influence.

It was erratic and swirling and played hideous tricks with the flight of the ball.

Town, however, despite the hostile conditions and Hartlepool's resolve, came from a goal down to win.

The result was, as the Leeds Road chief told me afterwards, "all that mattered".

"I always like to play well and win, but it's nice to play lousy for once and still win," he said. "That was our worst display of the season."

The worst or not, it was, in the final analysis, good enough to beat Hartlepool.

The story and anguish that followed might have been so different if Town had taken the lead after just three minutes. Peter Fletcher hurtled towards a Steve Kindon cross, but goalkeeper Graham Richardson blocked the header and sent the striker sprawling as the two men collided.

A goal then could have signalled a tremendous flourish but Town never settled into a convincing or penetrative rhythm.

Hartlepool, with three centre-backs casting as big a shadow over Town's effort as the main stand, also broke dangerously and twice Derek Hampton's left foot reminded Leeds Road that the visitors could play a bit as well.

After 22 minutes Ian Robins dropped a header on to the roof of Richardson's net and on the half-hour the goalkeeper rescued his side when Bernard Purdie seemed poised to score his first-ever goal for the club.

Richardson smothered the ball at Purdie's feet and the save was a prelude to Hartlepool taking the lead after 38 minutes.

John Linacre, who missed the team coach earlier in the morning and motored down the A1 himself, showed somewhat better timing.

Keith Hanvey's tackled halted Hampton's progress on the edge of the penalty area, but as the ball spun free, Linacre lofted it wide of Andy Rankin.

A hushed Leeds Road broke its silence as Purdie engineered another forward sortie, but seconds before the interval that man Hampton connected nicely with a low shot, the ball skipping wide of Rankin's right-hand post.

Town resumed with Dave Cowling replacing a concussed

FLASHBACK

TWELVE months earlier, [...] been beaten 2-0 by Hartle[...] penultimate match of 1978[...] Now, they were set to end [...] heartache during which the[...] dropped form the top flight [...] basement division.

Although promotion to Div[...] already been clinched, man[...] Buxton desperately wanted [...] take the Fourth Division t[...] century of League goals (t[...] going into this game).

The biggest home gate of t[...] 16,807, turned out to hail [...]

Dave Sutton — "I felt as though I had been hit by a brick and there was no way I could carry on," he said later — and Peter Hart switching to the centre of the defence.

Within an instant, though — for the statisticians the precise time was 47min 12sec — Town were level and the fans were saluting the team's 100th goal of the campaign.

Hanvey powered down the right,

nodded the bouncing ball forward and continued his charge to the byline where he whipped the ball across the face of the Hartlepool goal. From within a forest of legs Robins plunged headlong to direct it over the line and he emerged triumphant from a confused cluster of bodies.

Cowling, who swiftly began to stamp his authority in midfield, twice went close to scoring while

Hampton — who else? — could have restored Hartlepool's lead in the 67th minute when Rankin palmed Linacre's corner straight to his feet.

Finally, with nine minutes remaining and Walsall trailing to rampant Newport, Town went in front.

Another prodigious throw from Hart propelled the ball on to the head of defender Steve Brooks who

unwittingly guid[...] crossbar. Wit[...] grasping air, Rob[...] ball beyond him[...] aplomb.

Town, Rankin[...] Stanton, Sutton (Cowl[...] Laurick, Hart, Kindon[...] Hartlepool, Richardson[...] Hogan, Harding[...] Hutchen, Harding[...]
Sturart[...]
Referee — J B Worrall (W[...]
Attendance 16,807
Town man-of-the-match [...]

The Examiner provided unrivalled coverage of Town throughout their epic season.

FINAL LEAGUE TABLE

SEASON 1979–80

DIVISION IV

	P.	W.	L.	D.	Goals For	Ag.	Pts.
Huddersfield Town ..	46	27	7	12	101	48	66
Walsall	46	23	5	18	75	47	64
Newport County	46	27	12	7	83	50	61
Portsmouth	46	24	10	12	91	49	60
Bradford City	46	24	10	12	77	50	60
Wigan Athletic.......	46	21	12	13	76	61	55
Lincoln City	46	18	11	17	64	42	53
Peterborough United	46	21	15	10	58	47	52
Torquay United......	46	14	20	12	70	69	47
Aldershot	46	16	17	13	62	53	45
A.F.C. Bournemouth	46	13	15	18	52	51	44
Doncaster Rovers ...	46	15	17	14	62	63	44
Northampton Town .	46	16	18	12	51	66	44
Scunthorpe United ..	46	14	17	15	58	75	43
Tranmere Rovers	46	14	19	13	50	56	41
Stockport County ...	46	14	20	12	48	72	40
York City	46	14	21	11	65	82	39
Halifax Town	46	13	20	13	46	72	39
Hartlepool United ...	46	14	22	10	59	64	38
Port Vale	46	12	22	12	56	70	36
Hereford United	46	11	21	14	38	52	36
Darlington	46	9	20	17	50	74	35
Crewe Alexandra	46	11	22	13	35	68	35
Rochdale	46	7	26	13	33	79	27

What they said

Town chairman Keith Longbottom

"Since 1975 there has been an awful lot of frustration and aggravation. So I am delighted for everyone connected with the club that things appear to be coming right.

"To me personally the success this season means all the effort has not been wasted. Indeed, I owe a debt of gratitude to the manager, players, secretary, all the other staff and my fellow directors. The manager speaks his mind and we do as well but we all work as a unit."

Town manager Mick Buxton

"I like to win in style and you just have to look at the number of goals scored to see we did that. I don't want to appear bigheaded or put stupid pressure on myself, but I always said that if I couldn't get a team out of the Fourth Division then I would jack the job in. I am thrilled to bit for the directors. They have backed me to the full and at no time have they gone against me."

Town skipper Peter Hart

Promotion is the most important thing that has happened to me or this club in 10 years. What we have achieved won't really sink in until next August when we actually play against Division Three sides."

Town centre-half Keith Hanvey

"This promotion campaign is the highlight of my career. I'm just so glad to have been part of it. After so many disappointments, I didn't think success would ever come to me. It wasn't a lack of confidence but I just believed everything would pass me by."

Former Town manager Bill Shankly

"The manager has done well. He says what he thinks and I'm glad to hear that. A manager has to speak in a positive manner and continue to be his own man. Now they must try to avoid selling good players."

Former Town defender Trevor Cherry

"Mick Buxton has done a tremendous job and I don't think people realise how well he has done. He has changed the team quite a bit since Tom Johnston's day and has really worked wonders."

Mayor of Kirklees Cllr Donald White

"I have supported Town for many years through the good times and the not-so-good and have witnessed many exciting moments.

"However, I can honestly say that the current season has given me as much pleasure as any since I began watching from the terraces as a small boy.

"Over Easter, I was invited to travel on the team coach to Darlington when I saw at close quarters the wonderful team spirit, infectious enthusiasm and quiet confidence which ran through the whole party from directors to the driver."

First team coach John Haselden

"The realisation we were heading in the right direction came last season. We needed two or three new players, we got them and without being conceited it comes as no surprise to me that the team has done so well.

"We got rid of the idiots and now have a squad of players equal to any in the Third Division in terms of attitude, application and skill.

"We have our own personalities but Mick and I have an excellent relationship. We have the same approach to football and how it should be played.

"We more or less see players in the same light and never argue about anything. Having said that, if we did have a disagreement, whatever Mick says would go.

Town secretary George Binns

"I have said many times this season that success is due to a team effort from the players, the coaching staff, administrative people, maintenance and cleaning staff, pools staff and agents and the board of directors. For the first time in 10 years we have turned the corner and are heading in the right direction."

Huddersfield Daily Examiner soccer correspondent Paul Clark

"After a decade of disaster and disappointment, Huddersfield Town can at last bask in the glory of promotion. The ominous decline has been arrested and optimism is at an all-time high. For that we are indebted to the inspirational leadership of Mick Buxton and the relentless fighting spirit, courage and skill of his players.

"Town conquered the Fourth Division with a potent fusion of freedom and fluency which won the admiration of supporters from Bournemouth to Bradford, from Torquay to Tranmere. In all 46 games, Buxton sent his players into combat pledged to attack. And attack they did with relish and such rampant strength that they smashed more than a century of goals."

Former Town manager Ian Greaves

"I have seen them many times and they are very good to watch. Not only have they won the championship but they have won it in style. One of the problems at Huddersfield is producing enough money to buy players because not enough people come through the turnstiles. Mick will have to show his true colours when it comes to buying and selling."

The view from the dressing room

Town pen portraits by Brian Stanton

Alan Starling

Position: Goalkeeper

Born: Dagenham, 2 April 1951

Town appearances: 112

Our honorary Southerner always had an answer for everything. Everything ended up with a giggle with Alan because he was so jovial. He wasn't the best trainer in the world because that wasn't his forte. He was very old school. 'Why should I have to put in the hard yards when I only have to move a few yards to kick a ball in the six-yard box?' That summed up his mentality. There was no way he was going to break his neck but nevertheless he was a really good goalie.

Andy Rankin

Position: Goalkeeper

Born: Bootle, 11 May 1944

Town appearances: 81

Like me, he's from Liverpool and we got on really well because you often link up with people from the same neck of the woods. A very softly-spoken, funny man with a lovely dry sense of humour. He'd sit quietly in the corner of the dressing room and always chip in with the odd quip and like most Scousers, he'd always have some great stories. Plus, he was ultra reliable and unflappable as a goalkeeper.

Malcolm Brown

Position: Right-back

Born: Salford, 13 December 1956

Town appearances: 403 (23 goals)

He was the best player we had. He gave us so much. Never missed a game and thank God for that. He was really fast, great going forward, but he could defend as well. He had everything in his locker and I was there to make sure he could fulfill his attacking potential. He was destined for great things until he suffered his Achilles injury at Newcastle. Quiet, didn't say a great deal and just got on with the job, but a really terrific professional.

Dave Sutton

Position: Centre-half

Born: Tarleton, near Preston, 21 January 1959

Town appearances: 284 (15 goals)

One of the most honest and reliable people and one of the nicest guys to have played the game. A brilliant centre-half that you could never shut up. If a ball came into the penalty box and Sutty wasn't on the end of it, you'd be surprised. He put his head, at times, where he shouldn't have. He was brave. A good driving force, he was always talking, encouraging and pushing people. Very fit. Never stopped laughing. Great to be with.

Keith Hanvey

Position: Centre-back

Born: Manchester, 18 January 1952

Town appearances: 235 (15 goals)

Another very funny fella but with a deadly serious side to him as well and we called him 'Bamber' because he was so well educated. The one we'd go to if we had any problems with the club, like training methods or financial matters. He was our PFA (Professional Footballers' Association) rep because he was very diplomatic. Good talker and very intelligent off the field and on it. Very comfortable on the ball. Good organiser.

Chris Topping

Position: Centre-back

Born: Selby, 6 March 1951

Town appearances: 43 (1 goal)

He was Mr Polite. He'd be one of the players who'd say to me 'Brian, can you just go over there and mark this man?' I doubt Chris ever swore at anyone or cursed at anything in his life. But from a team point of view you knew if one of the regular centre-halves wasn't playing it would be no problem because Chris was coming in and he was so commanding in the air and trustworthy on the ground.

Fred Robinson

Position: Left-back

Born: Rotherham, 29 December 1954

Town appearances: 84 (2 goals)

As funny as he was hard which is saying something. As far as he was concerned, there was a lot in that old football saying that the 'ball might go past him, the player might go past him, but never both together.' Fred's style of play was hit them early and let them know you're there. He'd take no prisoners. There was no messing about with Fred. He was a non-nonsense defender could play as well. He was in an unusual position, a right-footed player at left-back but he made it look easy.

Bernard Purdie

Position: Utility player

Born: Wrexham, 20 April 1949

Town appearances: 46 (1 goal)

We crossed swords when we played Crewe and he was marking me. There were a few in. It wasn't nasty. He was a strong, form player. No one would have got an easy game against him. He was one of these players who got on with his job without much of a fuss. In most cases, you wouldn't know he was around. Very quiet.

Mick Laverick

Position: Central midfield

Born: Castle Eden, County Durham, 13 March 1954

Town appearances: 88 (12 goals)

He was like the spring in the watch. The one who kept everything moving around him. He kept us in-synch. A give-and-go player who was totally dependable. He played every game for us bar one that season but I can't remember him putting in a single below-par display. He'd get the ball and move it around without much fuss because he was a good reader of the game. One of the club comedians. Would always throw in one-liners.

Peter Hart

Position: Defender/midfield

Born: Mexborough, 14 August 1957

Town appearances: 229 (8 goals)

Like all good captains, Pete led by example and never shirked a challenge, which was just as well because he was there to break things up for us when our opponents were in possession. Good on the ball, a good short passer, he also popped up with a goal every now and again. I was surprised he left us for Walsall. He still had a lot to offer. Not a good move by him. I was sad to see him go but he did well.

Dave Cowling

Position: Left wing

Born: Doncaster, 27 November 1958

Town appearances: 393 (48 goals)

The amount of stick Dave got from the crowd was so unwarranted. He was the youngest member of the squad and we were amazed at why he got such much of it. He may not have been the bravest of players but he could hit a hell of a cross without any messing about which our forwards really appreciated. I just wish there had been the statistics available to illustrate how many assists he was responsible for. Very under-rated. Reasonably quiet off the field. Like me, he might not have been the life and soul of the place but he mingled well. Very consistent, hard-working with a great engine.

Ian Robins

Position: Striker

Born: Bury, 22 February 1952

Town appearances: 186 (67 goals)

I played with Ian at Bury where he did okay but they played him in midfield, which was puzzling. He made up for lost time at Town when he was finally restored to his rightful position as a striker because he had a gift for sniffing out goals, being in the right place at the right time. A deadly finisher but there was a lot more to his game as well. You always knew you could play a ball up to him and it would stick, he'd hold off his marker and lay it off while Malcolm Brown or me made a run. Key to our patterns of play. He made our little triangles worked well.

Peter Fletcher

Position: Striker

Born: Manchester, 2 December 1953

Town appearances: 115 (45 goals)

I'd have hated to be one of those centre-halves who had to play against Peter because he was such an awkward customer, dead skinny and all arms and elbows. Gave us extra height in the box. He knew where the goal was but he wasn't scared to get stuck in. He took the arrival of Steve Kindon in his stride when he lost his place in the first team but showed great character by weighing in with important goals right to the very end. Off the field, Peter was absolutely hilarious - a real laugh-a-minute friend and teammate who always kept us all amused.

Steve Kindon

Position: Striker

Born: Warrington, 17 December 1950

Town appearances: 82 (37 goals)

A larger than life presence whose speed, size and determination made him a real handful. He was a real outlet if it was a matter of 'let's get rid' and he relished those situations. Off the field you couldn't shut him up. We used to take the Mickey out of him incessantly about his lisp but took it in good faith. Liked to dish things out but sometimes didn't take things as well you might think. He played some tricks on Keith Hanvey so Keith retaliated by getting Nellie (Thompson) to sew up the sleeves of his shirt. He went berserk which didn't go down well but we soon forgave him.

Timeline

How the 1979/80 Fourth Division title was won

August 18 – Goals from Ian Robins and skipper Peter Hart ensure Town get their campaigns off to a flying start with a comfortable 2-0 win over Aldershot but just 3,313 fans turn up to usher in the new season at Leeds Road.

August 25 – Town brush aside Doncaster 3-0 at Leeds Road. Goals from Ian Holmes, Dave Cowling and Ian Robins prompt *Huddersfield Daily Examiner* reporter Paul Clark to write: "The Fourth Division will ignore Huddersfield Town at their peril. Their emergence as a real threat to all teams with a design on promotion was again illustrated with this fine victory."

September 10 – After boosting his squad in the summer by bringing in midfielder Mick Laverick and left-back Fred Robinson, Town boss Buxton strengthens again by signing attacking midfielder Brian Stanton from Bury for £13,500.

September 18 – Former Town stalwart Steve Smith is appointed chief scout

September 22 – Port Vale are taken apart by rampant Town who record their biggest win in 27 years and highest score of the season with a 7-1 victory at Leeds Road thanks to goals from Peter Fletcher, Hart (2), Robins (2), Stanton and an own goal in front of 4,299 fans.

September 28 – Town reach the summit of the Fourth Division table for the first time as goals from Laverick and Hart secure a 2-1 win at Stockport.

October 13 – A crowd of 16,540 watched Portsmouth go top by sweeping aside Town 3-1 at Leeds Road thanks to goals from Joe Laidlaw (2) and Jeff Hemmerman, who was sent off for trying to kick Peter Hart.

'The luscious stage was set and the packed gallery assembled to acclaim the all-star top-of-the-table cast," *Examiner* soccer writer Paul Clark said. "Fresh from a succession of rave reviews, Town made their entrance to a spine-tingling reception. Then, inexplicably, as the curtain opened, they stumbled over a production that has brought the house down in both Stockport and Peterborough. Sadly, the show wasn't the one many had come to watch..... even Portsmouth delivered the punchline after 38 minutes when star of the afternoon Laidlaw upstaged the entire Huddersfield defence.'

October 15 – Soccer hooligans who ran wild at the weekend came under fire from a senior police officer in the *Examiner*. "These people cannot be called supporters – they simply want to cause trouble and spoil the game for others," said Supt Peter Coddington.

He was speaking following trouble which saw 29 fans arrested after brawls in and around the ground. Supporters from Portsmouth were in town from 10am and hundreds spent hours at a Leeds Road pub where the landlord praised their behaviour.

But rival gangs chased each other across the terraces and Town secretary George Binns commented: "It makes it very difficult to segregate fans when they all have blue and white scarves. The root of the trouble was the drinking over lunchtime."

October 15 – Full-back Jim Branagan left Town for Third Division side Blackburn in a £20,000 deal while Phil Sandercock, who was put on the transfer list at his own request in August, moved to Northampton for £10,000 that month.

October 27 – Former England Under-21 goalkeeper Dick Taylor is taken to hospital after suffering a back injury while playing for Town's reserves.

November 7 – 'Town go nap as they go clear at the top,' said the *Examiner* back-page headline as 6,552 fans see the Terriers regain the lead in the promotion race by two points from Pompey after hammering Northampton 5-0 with goals from 'master executioner' Robins (2), Laverick, Cowling and Sutton. 'Casting a cursory glance over their shoulders, Town last night issued a catch-us-if-you-can challenge to the rest of the Fourth Division in extravagant style,' reported the *Examiner*.

November 17 – After a 1-1 draw with Tranmere, Buxton describes the visitors as a "disgrace" and added: "I feel sorry for the spectators. There was only one team out there that wanted to play. They were cheated."

December 3 – Goalkeeper Andy Rankin joins Town on a month's loan from Watford after Alan Starling suffers a rib injury.

December 18 – Steve Kindon says "no" to a transfer to Huddersfield and it is confirmed that Taylor needs back surgery.

December 21 – Kindon has a change of heart and agrees to join Town late in the night after watching a 5-1 Friday evening defeat of Rochdale at Leeds Road, which sees Rankin make his Terriers debut.

December 29 – Kindon marks his full debut for Town with the winner as Doncaster are beaten 2-1 at Belle Vue. Rovers manager Billy Bremner gives Town his seal of approval. "They are a good side but they showed a work ethic that my players will need to match if we are to challenge for promotion."

January 5 – 'Leaders pay for penalty miss as Kindon's last-gasp goal helps Town snatch a point,' was the *Examiner* headline after a 1-1 draw at pacesetting Walsall. The match report stated: "Walsall's performance – before their biggest crowd of the season (9,898) – was brimming with attacking flair and midfield vision while Town's was of the more basic qualities of resilience and diligence."

Walsall player-manager Alan Buckley missed a spot-kick but put his team ahead in the 77th minute before Kindon came to Town's rescue in injury time when he buried a low shot beyond goalkeeper Ron Green. "That goal was well worth waiting for," said Kindon while Buxton added: "Their goal was one of the best that's ever been scored against us. It would have been easy for us to drop our heads but we showed a lot of character to come back."

February 7 Buxton blasts the FA's two-match ban for Fred Robinson for reaching 23 disciplinary points, stating: "We have come to a very sorry state of affairs."

February 16 – 'Brian Stanton emerged triumphant from the Leeds Road dressing room on Saturday sporting a broad grin and the match ball tucked safely under his arm," reported the *Examiner* after a 5-0 win over Stockport.

"It was his hat-rick - the first of his career – that stole the show for Town on an afternoon when little appeared to be going right. A goal up after 19 minutes they should have railroaded Stockport but it just didn't happen. Their imagination was blurred, their cutting edge dulled.

'The transformation came after some harsh, no-nonsense words were delivered by Mick Buxton at half-time and suddenly the promotion spirit and adrenalin began to surge through their veins.'

"I told the players they were like a bunch of ballet dancers, 11 Nureyevs on stage," Buxton said. "That's not my way of playing and I cracked the whip. You've got to work and fight; nothing comes easy."

February 17 – The day after a 5-0 win over Stockport, Town fly to Guernsey for their first break in seven months to prepare for the crunch clash at Portsmouth. "You become a wee bit bored by the same routine," Buxton said. "The main thing is that we have a change of surroundings. Let's face it, most workers have a fortnight or so off at Christmas to enjoy something different. Now it's our turn."

February 19 – Buxton announces that he has signed a new contract during the trip to Guernsey when sightseeing, golf and a visit to a children's home are also on the players' itinerary.

February 23 – There was a surprising response from manager Mick Buxton's to Town heaviest league defeat of the season when they were stuffed 4-1 by Portsmouth at Fratton Park as David Gregory (2) Terry Brisley and Alan Rogers score for Pompey and Steve Kindon replies from the penalty spot.

"Keith Hanvey told me they expected a right rollicking and he couldn't believe what I said to them," Buxton said. "I told the players I'd never seen them play so well and that if they played like that for the rest of the season we'd definitely get promoted.

"I was upbeat because you have to look at the performance rather than the result. We played well but we lost. Individual mistakes cost us against a good team. I meant every word of it and I was proved right because we didn't lose another game."

February 25 – "Obviously our aim is to win promotion," Buxton told the *Examiner*. "But I would still like to finish the season as champions so it's important we bounce back." Maurice Porter announces planned launch of new Town lottery.

March 8 – 'If Town needed a result to underline promotion pedigree this was it,' the *Examiner* reflected. "Their victory at Bootham Crescent was cool, clinical and comprehensive. Four goals, 17 places and about a million miles was the gulf between York and a Town side that displayed ruthless efficiency. A win away from home was perhaps a little overdue - the last was at Doncaster on December 29 – but it was certainly worth waiting for. "We didn't just win, we won in style," said two-goal hero Steve Kindon.

March 29 – "Even the Brazilians wouldn't have fancied running about on that," said Mick Buxton after a 0-0 draw at Tranmere's Prenton Park ground where the pitch was described as "cloying, clinging and tugging at the ankles of the 22 players by Paul Clark. "That's the best advertisement for summer soccer I've seen,"

Buxton added. "It's very easy to be critical for there were many mistakes but when you look at the ground, well...." Andy Rankin was named *Examiner* man of the match while defeats for Walsall, Portsmouth and Bradford raised Town spirits.

April 5 'The fans filed away from Leeds Road happy with the five-goal Easter fiesta but unaware of the inner torment they had left behind,' reported the *Examiner*.

'Backstage, with the afternoon's rejoicing almost still audible around the stadium, there were no smiles on the face of manager Mick Buxton.

The sunny April day is also one best forgotten by Dave Cowling, the 20-year-old midfield terrier who failed to re-appear at half-time. Everyone was asking two questions: had Cowing been injured or had Buxton, after witnessing a goalless first half, finally given the supporters what they had been demanding for three months .... Kindon, Robins and Fletcher in a three-pronged attack?

"They gave him stick every time he got the ball," said Buxton. "Of course it influenced my decision at half-time to take him off. The lad was destroyed and it didn't help our game. For the first time in my career I have had to do something like this and it annoys me. Dave is normally a bubbly type of character but this has all gone. It knocked the shine off the victory and the players are as upset as I am."

April 12 – A crowd of 17,233 – Town's biggest home crowd all season - saw title favourites Walsall keep their nearest rivals at arm's length as Brian Stanton's first-half goal was cancelled out by Don Penn after the break when Town players had failed to heed a message chalked on a blackboard by Mick Buxton which said: 'Why are Walsall at the top of the league? Because they keep going.'

"We stopped competing," Buxton said. "For some reason the players thought they had won the match. In 15 minutes of the second half we virtually threw away any chance of the championship. They were warned and they have to learn and learn quickly."

Walsall boss Alan Buckley said: "It was a hard, physical game in bumpy conditions which we are not used to but the supporters got good value for money. We shall be playing Huddersfield in the Third Division, there's no doubt about that."

April 15 - A 10,900 crowd saw promotion effectively sealed at Leeds Road, with Ian Robins scoring both goals as Town beat Scunthorpe 2-1 to move to within three points of leaders Walsall with three games to go. The final whistle was greeted by a pitch invasion while Buxton hailed Town's board while sipping celebratory whisky.

"They have backed me to the full and even though I'm not a 'name' manager, they have never gone against me," said Buxton. "The best place to clinch promotion is here at home, in front of our fabulous supporters who have stuck with the club through the thin times.

"There's a hell of a lot of spirit here and we must keep going and advance further because these fans deserve success. The players will get a day off, but they have to report back ready to knuckle down, because our season isn't finished by a long chalk."

April 19 – Town formally end their five-year stretch in the Football League's basement division with a 3-1 at Hereford's Edgar Street ground courtesy of Peter Fletcher's brace and a goal from Steve Kindon

May 3 – The players who have steered Town to their first triumph in ten years enjoyed a rapturous salute on Saturday. As they completed their lap of honour around Leeds Road – where they have scored 61 of their 101 goals – the applause and cheers were long, sweet and warm. For the club's leading marksman, Ian Robins – who finished the season with a personal haul of 27 goals – was the added prestige of claiming the magical 100th goal. "I was delighted to have scored it but it didn't really matter who did," he said. "It was an important goal that put us back in the game."

Acknowledgements

Like a lot of the best attacking moves during the Mick Buxton era, the ball really started rolling on *The 101 Club* because of Brian Stanton.

I had often wondered whether the side that won the Fourth Division title had what it took for a book, but speaking to Town's former attacking midfielder confirmed it certainly was.

I had been asked by Town media chief David Threlfall-Sykes to interview Brian for the matchday programme *GUAH* to help spread the word about his plans to tackle the Great Manchester Run for charity.

That assignment reminded me what a golden era the Buxton years were for Huddersfield and so I owe him – and David – a special thanks for kicking this off and putting a good word in for me with the manager and all the other 15 players he used in the league that season.

The players – and their loved ones – deserve my gratitude for having to patience to help me piece together events before, during and after their time at Huddersfield and for speaking out for openly and honestly.

George Binns, the former Town secretary, was not only great company but he has also helped me check facts as well which has been vital as he is blessed with an encyclopedic brain.

The 101 Club could not have become a reality but for the support of Huddersfield Town Football Club and so I am especially grateful for the backing of commercial director Sean Jarvis, retail manager Luke Cowan and (to give him his full title) head of marketing and communications David Threlfall-Sykes.

Town supporter Andy Shuter has also played a crucial roles in turning my plans for this book into a reality by not only writing a chapter but for helping me get the club on board with this project.

I have to say a big 'thank-you' to David Burrill at Great Northern Books for backing my vision for *The 101 Club* with such enthusiasm from the word 'go' and for his guidance along the way and for designing a cracking cover.

My thanks also go to long-serving Huddersfield MP Barry Sheerman for taking the time out during his summer holiday to complete a fascinating chapter for this book to put the football club and the 1979/80 season into a social and historical perspective.

I am also grateful to the lovely members of staff at the Huddersfield Local Studies Library for helping my research on my trips back up to my hometown as I scoured their shelves and Microfiche machines.

Staff at the *Huddersfield Examiner*, *Yorkshire Post*, *Barnsley Chronicle* and *Rotherham Advertiser* have been important allies in my quest to get in touch with Town's former players as have the Professional Footballers' Association and the English Football League.

I would also like to give a special mention to Moor End High School (especially my French and Spanish teacher Barbara Ibanez) for helping me make the unlikely jump from Huddersfield's hardscrabble Walpole Road council estate to the press box at some of the biggest stages in football for *The Daily Telegraph*.

The way friends back in Huddersfield have encouraged me has been appreciated but the main source of help came from their parents, especially Christine and the much-missed Michael Harrison who encouraged me to set my sights on a career in journalism and Peter and Liz Turner who inspired me to become the first person on my estate to win a university place.

Last but certainly not least, thanks go to my family for putting up with me and the ups and downs of writing my first book and being a Huddersfield Town supporter and supporting this labour of love.

Rob Stewart
Bristol, October 2017.

Bibliography

Huddersfield Town – A Complete Record 1910-1990 (Terry Frost)

Huddersfield Town 75 Years On (George Binns)

Leeds Road – Home of My Dreams (Ian Thomas)

100 Years – All That's Worth Knowing. (George Binns, Alan Hodgson, Gwen and Ian Thomas)

The Daily Telegraph Football Chronicle (Norman Barrett)

Up There – The North East's Football Boom and Bust (Michael Walker)

Huddersfield Town matchday programmes

The Huddersfield Examiner

The Yorkshire Post

Terriers Fans

Eric Adams
Peter William Adams
Graham Airs
John Amitage
Roger Stuart Armitage
Harry Jack Aston
David Atkinson
Antony Bailey
Michael Barker
Simon Barker
Johnny Bartholet
Julian Bartholet
Francis Beardsell
Christopher Beaumont
Ian (bo) Beaumont
Paul Beaumont
Brian Bentley
Andy Berry
Neil Berry
Simon Berry
Daryl Blair
David Blakeley
Simon Blakey
Craig Blyth
Andy Booth
Elly Booth
Philip Booth
Stephen Booth
Paul Bootland
Paul Braithwaite UTT
Eddie Brammall
Neil Brammall
Dave Bray (Ossett)
David Broadhead
 Lee Broadhead
Granville Broadley
Daniel Brook
David Brook
Nigel Brook
Karen Brooke
Julian Brown
Malcolm Brown
Ian Bullock
Joshua Burgin
Sarah Burke

Keith & Sandra Burns
Nick Busby
Nick Carter
Dave Casson
Chris Chambers
Darren Clegg
Justin Cockcroft
Glen Cocker
R.M. Coldwell
John Collins
Nick Cooper
The Cran Family
Paul Crawshaw
Mark Croft
Martin Crossley
Gerald Crowther
Peter Daniel
Ross Daniel
Richard Dass
Ashley Derrick
Patrick Derrick
Mark Devenish
William Devenish
Barry Dixon
Paul Dobbin
Peter L Doherty
Alan Doyle
Billy Durrant
Bobby Dyson
Clark Eastwood
John Eaton
James Ellis
Steve Ellis
David Fenwick
Robert Firth
Shaun Fisher
Ray Francis
Mike Frier
John Garratt
Elizabeth M Garside
Marcus Garside
Brian Garton
Ibrahim George
Billy Gerrard
Paul Gerrard

Alan Gill
David Gill
Paul Gillespie
Phil Gooder
Kevin Gordge
Ben Green
Richard Green
Richard H Green
Warren Green
Steve Hadfield
Andrew Haigh
Irene Haigh
Dennis Hall.
Jack and Edith Hargreaves
Neil Hargreaves
Andy Hartley
Charles Hartley
Martin Hatfield
David, Heather
Chris Heeson
Chris Heley
Tim Heley
Chris Hepworth
Peter Hepworth
Philip Hewlett
Beverley Hey
Derek Hey
Stanley Hill
Ann Hillock
Bryan Hirst
Nigel Hitchborn
Clive Holt
Lee Holt
Julian Horbury
David Howard
Graham Hoyle
John Hoyle
David Hudson
John Hutchings
John D Jackson
Richard Jessop
Geoffrey Johnson
Graham Johnson
Simon PJ Johnson
Ian Kendall

Jerome Kennedy
David Kenworthy
Jeanette Kenworthy
Nigel Kenworthy
Andrew Kirk
Steven (kitty) Kitchen
Mark Knowles
Andrew Lemon
Mr Peter Lemon
Mick Lindley
Graham Lister
Ian Littlewood
David Lodge
Mick Loughrey
Brian Macer
Bill Maldzinski
Ian Marsden
John Mason
Ryan Mather
David Maugham
Steve Maugham
John McCallum
Neil Mellor
Steve Mellor
Steven Mellor
Geordie Mick
Paul Miller
Alan Milnes
John Mitton
Philip Mitton
Chris Moody
Xavier Dale Moorhouse
Lee Morris
Michael Mosley
Simon Neve
Richard Newton
Mark Nicholson
Ian Noble
Andy North
John O'Mahoney
John Oldroyd
Scott Oldroyd
Steven (Eddie) Oldroyd
Brian Oram

Roger Pashby
Phil Payne
PDJMHTFC
Raymond Peace
Richard Peace
Steve "Billy" Peckett
Robert Pepper
Asher Petch
Jonathan Petty
Pork Pie64
Steve Pogson
John L Poulter
Alec Priestley
Ray Pullen
Malcolm Purdy
Andrew Raven
Mick Raven
John Read
Alan Rees
Charlie Rigg
John Robb
Jacob Roberts
Clive Robinson
Robert Robinson
Paul Schreibke
Mike Shackleton
Brian Shears
Darren Shears
james Sill
Paul Skilbeck
Graham and John Smith
Ian Barry Smith
Jock Smith
John D Smith
Kieran Smith
Paul K Smith
Rob Smith
Peter Stansfield
Andrew Stead
Chris Stead
Rob Stead (Oscarbravo)
Paul Stephenson
Iain Stevenson
Mick Suddaby

Darren Sykes
Paul Sykes
Stuart Tattersfield
Beverley Anne Taylor
Kevin Taylor
Mary Taylor
Mr Jason M Taylor
Andy Thewlis
Neil Thomas
J.C.Thompson
John Charles Thompson
Paul Towers
Danny Tyndall
John Tyndall
Raymond Valat
Clive Waddington
Steven Wadsworth
Janet Walker
John & Pauline Waller
Richard Waller
Helen Walsh
Paul Walton
A.C.Warden
M.J.Warden
Andrew Warren
Craig Waterworth
Robert Waterworth
David Watson
Bill Watt
Ian K Whitehead
Martin Whiteley
Nick Wilding
Reverend David Wilding
Joseph Wilson
David Alan Wood
Ed Wood
Nicky & Jason Wood
Mel Woods
Alan Fraser Wrigley
Bryn and Ciaran
Mark
Queenie